To Bishop
Salara Mawin Jr.

What is Lost?

you light!!

Thank you
for your support
Both Spiritual & Natural!
Thank God
for You ? You
bring

05/03/2001

Bishop Mawin Jr.

What Is Life

KEVIN WASHINGTON

ATO PUBLISHING
"AND THEY OVERCAME..."

ISBN: 978-0-578-76720-8
For Worldwide Distribution, Printed in the U.S.A.

DISCLAIMER

While this memoir is a work of non-fiction, some names,
places and events have been altered to respect the right
to privacy of all citizens.

AUTHOR CONTACT INFORMATION

Kevin Washington

lordcdo@gmail.com

717-439-1220

CONTENTS

ACKNOWLEDGEMENTS

ATO Publishing (And They Overcame)
Founder: Author Teresa Collins

Cover Layout & Design:
Wow Factor Studios - 815-483-8435

Editorial Director:
David Collins

Musical References:
Precious Lord Take My Hand (1932) by Thomas A. Dorsey
Turn Off the Lights (1979) by Teddy Pendagrass
Victory In Jesus (1939) by Eugene Monroe Bartlett
I Did It My Way (19xx) Sammy Davis, Jr.

Oral Traditions:
Mrs. Jacynthia A. Robinson-Washington

Famous Quotes:
Words like doors open with ease, spoken by Jacynthia A. Robinson-Washington, inspired by the famous quote, Hearts like doors will open with ease, by Anonymous Author – (1936)

Pre-publication Content Review and Feedback:
Terrance Patillo

Poetic Contributions
TC The Artist – Our Love
Teresa Collins – Waiting

Scriptural References:
AKJV of The Word of God

Living with a Life Changing Accident References:
Google.com

Kevin Washington Becomes First Black CEO

Letting-Go, LLC, L.O.R.D. Community Development
Organization, Inc. and Washington Associates. He is the
Pastor of Unity Fellowship Church of God in Christ.

L.O.R.D. News Report
Written April 19, 2015

Kevin Washington, is the first African-American CEO
of the following organizations, Letting-Go, LLC, Launching Out
Reaching Deep, Washington Associates, and Pastor of Unity
Fellowship Church of God in Christ.

This marks yet another "first" achievement for the
Harrisburg leader, as he becomes the first African-American
to hold the position.

"Kevin brings deep and varied Community experience and a strong record of accomplishment on behalf of communities he has served. His business growth — which he has been building toward his entire career," said the organizations are a statement. "He is an exceptional cause-driven leader who is committed to Community Mental Health. Strategic direction is to become a national provider."

Known for his unconventional methods and strategic mindset, Washington has risen through the ranks of the Human Service field since becoming a youth counselor in 1987.

His many career highlights thus far include providing quality service through his organizations to more than 15,000 households in the greater Harrisburg Area, L.O.R.D. News reported.

Washington also credits his mentor, Mr. James A. Jones, for his professional experience both as an athlete and businessman. Jones began mentoring Washington since he was 19 years old.

His knowledge of business development has shaped "Washington the adolescent to Washington the adult".

"I tell everyone Success Disguises Itself Through Hard Work."

Reviews

"What Is Life" by Kevin N. Washington, Sr. is an extraordinary account of a man overcoming tremendous odds against him after being involved in a head on collision car accident that left him paralyzed. Through his faith, determination, and perseverance, he was able to overcome all the doctor's prognosis that he would never walk or have kids, to not only walk, but marry and fathered four children. Kevin N. Washington, Sr., is a hero to all that need an example of victory in life!

Superintendent James S. Gamble, Sr.
Eastern Jurisdiction of Pennsylvania
Church of God in Christ

I've known Kevin since the early 70's and we became the best of friends over the years. When I heard he was in a devastating auto accident and was paralyzed it was a total shock and hard to imagine. Throughout several conversations after the accident, he was adamant that he was going to walk again and live a fully functional life. I can clearly remember pushing Kevin in a wheel chair and when I look at him now, it is obvious that it was the grace of God and his determination that he is living that fully functional life he talked about. Congratulations and Love you brother!

Tom Williams

***

God's plan is better than anything we can imagine. To witness Mr. Washington relentless, unstoppable, undeniable, faith in God is impeccable to the community he serves. He took the lemons that were thrown his way and created a lemon cake, lemonade, and a lemon pie. Life has its challenges and peaks and valleys, but nothing can compare to a man who surrenders his all to God. He is a master swordsman that uses his gifts God gave him to serve others. No wonder God had others plans for him to become a walking masterpiece, as you will experience when you purchase your copy of his memoir, "What is Life."

Natasha Harris
CEO of Broken Wings Literacy Center

***

"Pastor Kevin Washington has displayed exceptional courage under extreme circumstances. I am sure that his book will be an encouragement to anyone who reads it."

Pastor Joseph B. Turner

***

Pastor Kevin Washington, What an honor to know you and witness what God has done, and is doing at this present time in your life. God is showing his love and miraculous healing power through you. You are soaring like an eagle in faith and love for God, Family, Church, and Community. You are a Blessed Servant of God and a Blessing! "Love and Prayers"

Your Spiritual Mother S. M. Baltimore, Carter

***

Kevin Washington AKA (Special K) the author is a great man that is a father, husband, pastor and a leader in the community. I have been knowing Kevin since 1980 we first met on the football field at Cheyney University. Kevin transferred from Lock Haven University, the team that defeated us in the championship the year before. So, you know he was a hated man on the field and on campus. This did not last long...He became one of the leaders on and off the field. Unfortunately, Kevin was seriously injured in a car accident that ended his promising football career. We all were saddened by this tragic event but as usual it did not stop Kevin from being successful in life. God took over in Kevin's life and captured his true love for humanity and he has rescued, helped, nurtured and developed individuals to success. I can testify to this because, I am one of the individuals he assisted along my journey in life!!! I would like to thank him personally for his support spiritually and professionally, my main man Special K!!!! Congrats with your book, man!

Darryl C. Overton
A Philip Randolph High School
Principal and Friend

***

Life is simple yet complexed. This appears to be part of God's glory. We go through experiences some good, some bad, yet we find oneness in all we do. Like all of God's creation Kevin's story is a living testimony to how God works. He was struck down and raised again by God's grace. My relationship with Kevin has blessed me beyond words. Give thanks and praise.

James Jimmy Jones

My Wife and Children

(F) Thelma, (B) Te'ressa, Kevin – KJ, Kalann, (M) Karrington

Special Recognition

I would like to recognize, acknowledge, and
applaud my greatest support system:

Faith, Family, & Friends

MY CREATOR:
The Father, The Son, The Holy Spirit

MY FRIENDS:
Tommy, Ray, Sam, Andrew

MY COUSINS:
Shawn, Jay C – Boomie, Elves – Grit, Stanley – Oil
Can, The Twins: Don & Ron, Stevie – The Prince of
Gospel

In Loving Memory

- John N. Robinson, Grandfather
- Marion Jackson – Robinson, Grandmother
- Catherine Robinson – Burton, Great Aunt
- Reginald A. Washington, Biological Father
- Jacynthia A. Robinson – Washington – Cormack, Mother
- Robert Keith, Father
- Shauna Cormack, Sister

Dedication

Thelma, my wife, my rib, my soulmate:
You are incomparable, incredible, irreplaceable.
You are an unmatched, invaluable, God-given gift
to me. Your outward splendor is equaled only by
your inward elegance and charm. Yes! You have
been well-favored. And yes, you still take my
breath away. You are my heart; my box of wine
palm sweets. Your heart is mine. You have devoted
each beat to me on a plateau I had once only
longed for. You have loved me, and I love you,
deeply, lushly, endlessly. Your love pours upon my
heart as welcomingly as a long awaited rain. Your
love, my dove, is the sweetest, sappiest, dewiest
delicacy any man can possess. You meet challenge
and setback with wings of faith spread forth as

broad as the mustard tree, transforming our pain, miniscule or mighty, into power simply with the tender touch of your hand gliding across the left side of my face...

As we continue our life together, simply enjoy the wind that blows through your hair, always remembering, come what may, as long as we face it together!

Till my parting breath,

Your husband, man, lover, and friend

Elder Kevin Washington

FOREWORD

What is Life, presents an autobiographical account of events from Kevin N. Washington Sr., and chronicles his audacious journey. From poverty to standout student-athlete, from dysfunctional family to leading his own, and from professional football recruit to paralyzed college senior, Kevin's story of overcoming his battles with depression, anger, and trauma is a rollercoaster full of high heights and valley lows.

A graduate from one of the oldest Historically Black Colleges in the nation, Cheyney State University, Kevin received his Bachelor of Arts Degree in Psychology and Community Mental Health. He is a record setting football player and professional recruit. Kevin's inspirational life-long trek for redemption, forgiveness, and wholeness keeps him grounded in humility. He leaves behind the world of fame, greed and selfish pride, and grabs hold to faith, marriage, ministry, and fatherhood. Kevin has risen above his past and has become a successful entrepreneur and businessman. He is a beacon light in his community, and is revered as a citizen of esteem.

What is Life, shares the intimate details of the tragedy, triumph, failure, and success of his journey. This is a story of relentless faith, purpose, passion, and inspiration to reach higher in the face of overwhelming odds. His story is truly a must read.

Kalann L. Washington
Graduate of Messiah College, Psychology Major

PROLOGUE

I was flying high; about to make some major moves in my life. I was the cream of the crop. I was moving around with the elites.

On the outside things were looking outstanding. The future was so bright and promising. But I did not realize then, like I realize now, I was becoming a double minded young man. I was on a clear path with a distorted vision. I was conflicted. It seemed that I was about to have what most men in this world fight their entire lives. While they were still searching, I had just about seized it. I almost had it in the palms of my hands. It was on the tip of my tongue waiting to fall from my lips. Everyone around me was so excited and enthusiastic about where my life was headed. The handshakes, the pats on the back, the go get 'em champs; I must admit that for a while it was exhilarating. But that was fizzling fast. It became a way that people could live out their fantasies on my fame.

As I look back and reminisce over my life when I was a child, I realize that the seed that God placed in my heart all those years ago had taken root and was beginning to bud. It was growing stronger. I could feel it. I developed an aching on the inside that would not go away. I began to long for words of exhortation that I received from the adults in my life as a child. I longed for The Word of God, for Sunday School. I longed for Sunday night service. I longed for whom my soul loved. I felt like the starry-eyed smitten lover in the Book of Ecclesiastes. I was searching for love in all the wrong places.

I heard a small, very still voice telling me that the way of fame and fortune was not for me. I began to realize that no matter how much money and popularity I acquired, it would not be satisfying, and my life would still be empty. Amidst all my shiny things, I was still empty. There was a hole in my heart. I no longer longed for the shiny things. I longed for the light that would shine on my soul.

My soul was in prison. A prison of pride. A prison of the desire for fame and fortune. A prison of people pleasing characteristics. And a prison of pride to be the most successful and adored athlete.

I worshipped the female creation more than I worshiped the Creator Himself. I was ashamed to be my true, authentic self. Living for God is what I truly wanted. It was not cool or popular; but still, it is what I wanted. I wanted to live for God.

If I chose God, I would no longer be revered as Teddy P – turn off the lights, Joe Wash, Special K, or The Chill Factor – because you might get frostbit. I felt like I would be nobody. No one would chant my name from the bleachers. No females would go to great lengths just to be in my presence. All eyes would be someplace else, and not on me. I WAS TORN. I didn't know how to give all that up. I wanted both worlds. I was truly at a crossroad.

I didn't want people to know that my soul really loved the Lord. It was like I was walking around with a dirty little secret.

I tried camouflaging it with popularity. I was the life of the party. I flirted a little harder, laughed a little louder, smiled a little brighter, and walked a little cooler than others. I immersed myself into the celebrity mindset and behavior. Yes, I had it down to a tee! I was Kevin Washington, Joe Wash, Teddy P, and The Chill. And everyone knew it. But what they did not know was my soul was locked up. And I was afraid to even look in the direction of the key.

So, those same parties that I was used to going to and loved so much, were becoming a ball and chain. It was a drudgery. I wasn't enjoying myself anymore. I wasn't enjoying life. I wasn't happy. I was sad. I was a sad man. When no one was around I was a crying man in a world of blind men. My friends did not see me. They did not see my pain. Many of them would approach me and say "Man... You see that hottie over there. I'm about to serve." I would look and say "You are a bad man, Bro. I wish I had run into her first." But, in reality, I didn't want that life anymore. I was glad that he ran into her first. My desires were changing. I was losing interest in that sort of thing, but still trying to hold on to my image at the same time. I began having to force myself to at least pretend that I was still in the game. And sometimes I participated in the game. But the rules were changing for me. How long will I have to play their game? How long will my soul have to be in prison? Will I ever get out?

Chapter 1

Destiny

"For I know the thoughts that I think toward you, saith the LORD, thoughts of peace, and not of evil, to give you an expected end..."
Jeremiah 29:11

The violent strength of the wind, the coercive rain beating against the submissive ground, the unrelenting darkness dominating the weeping sky, and the arduous weight of the time-honored car conspire with fate and collude with the narrowing two-lane road as the utterly oblivious drunken driver derails the trajectory of my life.

Suddenly, I found myself facing a sobering truth: *I should not have gotten in that car...*

***

We have been celebrating all week. The glitz and glam of our awaiting future are just a few weeks away.

"Kevin!" Jennifer yells excitedly up the stairs. "Come on, babe! We don't want to be late! Mom and Dad are already tucked away in Ms. Clarice Foxtail ready to go!"

I'm thinking, how can we be late? We're going to a Casino. But, whatever, it ain't no puzzle. And why is dad driving? The doctors said he can't drive. The old guy knows his vision is impaired! But, whatever, man, it aint no puzzle.

I run down the swirling staircase sporting my 'money-talks' equipment, dancing to the slickety-clickety sound of my Salvatore Ferragamo dark brown Italian soft leather monk strap high-top dress shoes while laying down the latest trend - my elongated collar on my finest Macy's white shirt, an added accessory to compliment my dark brown Ralph Lauren Polo lambswool pull-over sweater – all gifts from the hotties – total equipment cost $475 and change, head to toe. What can I say? The ladies love me. The lambswool is a hottie-stopper. It is soft on the body, just like the hotties. But as sharp as I am, I'm still not ripped about going to the casino.

"Jennifer, why don't you encourage your parents to pardon our absence so that you and I can spend some quality time alone. I would love to relax in front of the television with you and catch a great movie and maybe give you a little something to make it a night to remember." I give her my smoothest smoldering eyes and a devious grin and begin twisting my pelvis from side to side while beckoning her to come closer.

Jennifer gives me her look in return. "Hummmm! Not a bad idea, Babe. Your offer is so very tempting... buuuut, I know you wouldn't want me to let this beautiful dress and hairdo go to waste sitting around watching T.V., now would you?" She spins around flirtatiously showing off all her voluptuous curves that are hitting her body in all the right places. She does a very slow dance without taking her steamy eyes off me.

"Mmmmm," is the only sound that comes to my mind. I bite the corner of my lip. "Come here girl," I whisper.

She continues her salacious show, culminating with a sultry curtsey and a few suggestive arm raises the way a trained night club dancer does, showing off her sparkles and rhinestone earrings and necklace.

"Oooooowee, why is it so hot in here, girl? Did you turn the heat up to AFRICA!!! Got me over here sweating and all! Look at you, with your fine self. Come here, girl!"

She lets her eyes fall shyly and moves toward me. I wrap my hand around her waist and slowly pull her in the rest of the way.

"I guess you are right, girl. It's time for the world to see what I have. They can look, but never touch… like the way I'm about to touch you right now."

Our kiss is soft, passionate, and juicy. "Mmmm, girl… does this mean you are going outside to tell your parents to go on without us… you want me to finish what you started, right?" I take her hand and place it right where I want it…

"Ooooh, Kevin, you are a big bad boy!" She looks down at her hand and squeezes just enough. "But pleeeease, babe," she said in her "whiny, I want more" voice. Please don't tease me right now. You know how I get. She squeezed and released once more. It's time to go! Ooooh my goodness! Your offer is soooo tempting!"

"Squeeze it again."

"Babe, stoooop. We've got to go." She plants a soft, moist kiss on my top lip.

"I know. But you can't blame a guy for trying. I mean, look at you! All gorgeous. Got me going crazy. With a dress and a fine, delicious, tawdry body like yours, it's time to paint the night."

"Tawdry! Did you just call my body tawdry? I beg your pardon, sir."

I laugh. "You know you are irresistibly sexy when you are angry. You had better straighten up before I carry all this tawdriness back up those stairs and teach you a lesson."

"Boy please, you are not about to get none of this tawdry, aesthetically crafted behind! But you owe me big time, babe. And yes, I mean BIG time... And be ready to pay up tonight! I plan on winning the lottery! I'm hot!" She licks the tip of her finger and strokes herself on her backside as if striking a match.

I take her hand and place it back on her favorite part of me. "As you can see, I'm hot too! We don't have to wait until tonight. I can pay my debt right now, with a big bonus on the side…"

"Oouuu la la, such a naughty boy. Someone call the fire department because this boy is on fire! Let's go Prince Charming!"

I laugh and hold my arm out to escort my Princess to our awaiting chariot in the double wide, multiple car driveway, singing all the way…

Turn off the lights and light a candle
Tonight I'm in a romantic mood, yeah

Let's take a shower, shower together, yeah
I'll wash your body and you'll wash mine, yeah
Rub me down in some hot oils, baby, yeah
And I'll do the same thing to you

Just turn off the lights, come to me
Girl, I want to give you a special treat, you're so sweet

TURN EM' OFF…

"Wow babe! Isn't this exciting!"

"Well, I'm a lucky man. Now get all of that in this car so we don't keep your parents waiting any longer, plus the weather seems like it's about to get rowdy. We want to get there before it throws a tantrum." I open the door behind the driver's seat and stealthily get a few free feels while helping her into the car. I sigh deeply, look up to the sky, then trudge around to the passenger door.

After we arrive at the casino, and Jennifer and I step away from her parents, I ask, "So... Baby, what are we going to do about the distance between us? We will be attending two different colleges in two different states. We will be hundreds of miles apart. We won't be able to see each other very often. Are we up for this journey? Are we really ready? Can we do this?"

"Oh, babe, you worry too much. It will all work itself out. Let's concentrate on having a good time! We're here to party! I plan on winning at the slot machines! I think I'll spend big tonight and dedicate a whole $20 bill toward my fortune! It's going to be great! You'll see!"

"Ha, ha! A whole $20, Hun? Funny! I'd like to see you do that! But I'm serious, Jennifer. These are things we need to discuss. We only have a few weeks to figure it all out. I tried discussing it in the car but you kept changing the subject."

"Kevin, stop! You are killing my mood, baby! We are supposed to be celebrating, not discussing living arrangements. I don't care about any of that right now. All I care about tonight is this moment! I need you to lighten up. Stop being a worrywart," she says as she walks away trying to get change. "Excuse me, sir! Excuse me! May I have change for this $20 bill, please. All quarters." She smiles then waves the $20 bill above her head like it is a white flag rescuing her from my myriad of introspection.

This is not a good day for me. I'm walking around the Casino with my gut twisting in twin sets. My head is pounding, the stress is mounting, and Jennifer seems to be clueless to everything except the good time she keeps stuffing into the mouth of the slot machines and game tables. She's in her element. She doesn't have a second thought about the $800 she has already lost. Mixing and mingling with all the socialites and standing around watching the big spenders win and lose hundreds of thousands of dollars is the highlight of her night.

"Kev, give me a few more $20 bills, Babe. I promise I won't spend over $500 tonight!"

"Whatever," I mumble under my breath. As usual, she doesn't keep up with how much she is gambling. I don't say anything this time. I simply give her another wad of $20s.

"You should join in. I'm having a blast!"

My subdued smile pleases her. My mother-in-law seems content either way. My father-in-law takes great pride in introducing me to his rich lawyer friends and political officials in his pocket!

I smile and nod astutely, while shaking hands with the tycoons.

"Yeah, this is a fine young man," my father-in-law says. "I drove him here tonight to meet you. He's a great investment as a son-in-law! Wonderful person!"

The whole thing feels weird; like at the roll of the dice I would become the winnings of the highest roller. But I'm not going to panic. I suck it up...

The sound of the poker chips shuffling on
the clawing table,
The rhythm of the sexy hypnotic music,
Loud drunken cheers,

A cocktail of expensive perfumes swimming

through the air

Dark sunglasses,

Walkie-talkies,

Loaded hip holsters,

The pristine maître d,

Security at every exit and entrance,

Security lining the parking lots,

Security near the elevators,

Security lining the big spender's section,

Sweating foreheads,

Musty arm pits,

Swearing,

Cursing,

Profanity,

Security guards dragging out angry losers

Long stem glasses easing guilty consciences,

Shot glasses,

Bottles of beer,

Bottles of wine,

Rows and rows of jackpot machines,

Cha-chinging non-stop,

More swearing,

Security guards accosting and dragging out
more angry losers,

Lipstick on wine glasses,

Women with white gloves and clutch
purses,

Fat old men with skinny young girls wearing
next to nothing,

Dead gazes in the eyes of all the gamblers

Dead gazes in the eyes of all the workers

Swirling drinks in the hands of visiting
gamblers that must explain what happened
to the mortgage money,

And me.

My crawling skin.

I just want to get out of here.

"Jennifer…"

"Yeah, babe. Hey, I need more $20 bills…"

"I want to be saved. I want to give my life to
  God."

"What are you talking about, Kev? Did you hear me? I need more $20 bills."

I handed her another stack of $20 bills.

"Living for God, Jennifer."

Jennifer sighs...

"I don't understand, Kevin. What is your problem?"

"It's been on my mind for weeks."

"Okay..."

"It's time. You know how I always say that timing is everything. Well it's time."

"Kev, that's great. But we go to church... We are good people... What else is there? Do you want to take communion this Sunday? We can find a church that will be serving it, you know. Come on, go back with me to the tables. I want to play some more."

"Jennifer, listen to me, babe! Listen."

"No, Kevin, stop! I already told you, you worry too much! What is wrong with you? You're making a big deal out of nothing. You are a really good Christian! So am I; I have been taking communion since the age of five. I take it every Easter. Stop worrying, we're good! You're killing the mood with all this senseless jibber jabber. Now trust me, babe. Everything is going to work out. You'll see. Focus on the crap tables tonight. Let your hair down. Live a little!"

I smile halfheartedly. Underneath my breath I mumble, "You call this living. Whatever!"

"Great! Now loosen up! Let's get some of this money! Let's do it big tonight, babe! Yeah! Give me a few more $20 bills, this stack isn't big enough! I need more chips! We've arrived! You've been working for this your whole life and now we are here! You're on top of the world, baby! We're at the top! You're Kevin Washington! Special K! The Chill Factor! Enjoy it. Now, roll the dice! You're a winner. It's destiny!"

***

15

Chapter 2

The Accident

For what is your life? It is even a vapor, that appeareth for a little time, and then vanisheth away.

James 4:14 b-e

"Ms. Clarice Foxtail" is the pet name of my father-in-law's long, sleek Classic Mercedes-Benz 300SEL, and has been my father-in-law's other woman, and real true love for the past eleven years. After separating honorably from the military, one of his Army buddies shipped her to him from Stuttgart, Germany, straight from the showroom floor. He says she's a real

16

bargain; worth every penny he invested! Her strong V8 engine makes her a perfect race horse, and her classic body is prime for leisurely evenings with the family. She pleases my father-in-law; and assuredly, has been generous to him throughout the course of their eleven-year union as well. She's his silver fox with platinum packaging. He usually saves her for special occasions, one such as this, when he feels braggadocious and wants to flaunt both his women and his wallet. But tonight, proves to be a bit much on one of his girls. Ms. Clarice Foxtail is in turmoil.

Upended by adverse weather conditions, the recently rotated, top-of-the-line, white-wall Firestones have no other recourse but to pay obeisance to nature. Ms. Clarice Foxtail begins pirouetting insanely in the savagely villainous wind and fiendish rain. From the plush backseat of the prestigious car, I see a disquieting quivering of the lips consume the side of my

father-in-law's face before he utters those
unforgettable words...

"Oh Nooooooo!"

***

They say men are better drivers than
women. I don't know if that is a true statement or
just an erroneously chauvinistic claim to cause an
unnecessary clash and disharmony between men
and the wonderful species we love, the
descendants of Eve. I'm thinking...

*Here they go again; crazy teenagers! Gotta
love them, right? Driving recklessly and not paying
attention to the rules of the road... and in this
sinister weather... Stupid kids! It's ridiculous, right?*

I can't tell how fast the driver is driving but
the tiny headlights are growing bigger and more
blinding by the second.

*Do the rest of you see this lunacy? Or, is it
just me?* I'm in the back seat observing but growing
increasingly leery listening to the wheels
screeching and the engine revving!

That guy is nuts! It has to be some snotty nose, pimple faced teenager showing off for his girl in Daddy's Lamborghini! Crazy kid. Whatever! He'd better stay on his side of the road!

"Wooooah!" My eyes open as wide as a crock's mouth. *Is this really about to go down?* Before I could indulge my fellow blue hearted traveling compadres…

SWERVE…

BOOM!

My father-in-law's next words were spoken like a true sage… "CLARICE! WE'RE GONNA HIT!"

I brace myself, press my head hard into the cushion behind me, close my eyes tight and pray…

WHIRLING, WIZZING, SCREECHING, then CRASH…

***

My head is pounding like a hammer and nails. My thoughts are colliding. I lick my lips and taste blood and grime in my mouth. I attempt to lean forward so that I can eject the unsavory mixture. The seatbelt is in panic mode and will not release. I'm wondering what is going on. I wrap my bleeding fingers around the base of the strap holding me in an upright position, press the button and pull. And nothing. I tug on the strap and wriggle the buckle frantically, but again, nothing. It is locked in break position. I can feel a slippery sludge slithering down my chest toward my groin. I pat my chest up and down wondering, *Is this what I think it is...* I rub my marinating thumb back and forth across the tips of my remaining fingers to examine the gelatin gunk resembling the goo at the bottom of a roasted ham pan after the liquid cools.

The scent of burning rubber melting infuses the air. The sharpness of the odor annoys my nostrils. Metrically, I inhale in short rhythmic spurts. Sniff, sniff, sniff... Sniff, sniff, sniff... *Am I near a toy factory where they manufacture those hardened rubber figurines that usually get lost at the bottom of some kid's toy box?*

The trenchant taste of gas lingers behind the blackened rubber. I form my lips into the small letter "o" then make my stomach hard and cough up the taste of gas in my throat and underneath my tongue. Some of the grime glops out of my mouth and lands on my chin. I turn my head and raise my shoulder to wipe my chin against it. The fumes are real as the chunk of ham meat resting in the tasty goo at the bottom of the pan.

A slither of light cascades from the distant moon allowing me to see a subtle reflection in the rearview mirror of what appears to be a human visage. The awkward form staring back at me is unsettling.

"Who are you and what do you want?" My ears stand up straight like a dog's ears waiting for a reply. But nothing. The almost human visage says nothing. I stare numbly at the blank, charred face with reverence, pity, and fear.

Were my eyes playing tricks on me?

The night light is opaque, but his eyes are piercing, cutting clean through the stalking darkness. I stare at the ghoul without blinking to gain dominance. But my weakening eyes were no match for his monstrous over gaze. I drop my head in submission and look away shamefully. The hair on the back of my neck stands up. The stars are winking, and the sky cowers in disarrayed with iridescent clouds forming unfamiliar shapes in the near starless night giving the ogle the look of a chameleon.

Blurred judgement...

Blurred vision...

Blurred senses...

How did I get here?

***

"*Don't be proud, Charles. Give me the keys so that I can give them to Kevin. You know your eyes are not useful at night. You have trouble seeing the stirring wheel.*"

"Hush woman. I haven't been in an accident in how many years? Never years! That's how long! There is nothing wrong with my eyes! No one drives Ms. Clarice but me!"

"Why are you being stubborn, Charles?"

"Everyone in this family thinks I'm an imbecile? Like I can't drive. I've been driving longer than the lot of you put together. Driving at night... It's the same as driving in the day. It's the same thing. I'm not giving up my keys."

The warning was brisk, sharp, and too late. He didn't see it coming. He had no time to grip the leather-bound steering wheel tighter and whirl out of harm's way. For the first time in their eleven-year love affair, Ms. Clarice Foxtail felt vulnerable. Charles could not protect her. Her tires were already suspended just above the traction of the ground the way a hockey puck does when smacked across the icy arena floor. The calamitous crash was seismic. The beautiful lady, Ms. Clarice Foxtail, heaved in despair then emitted a shrilling cry.

* * *

I rub both my eyes with the balls of my
hands then look around trying to regain my
bearings and my sight, but pandemonium prevails.
The grayish smoke clouds my vision. Nothing is
making sense. And nothing is making a sound
except the rear end white walls whizzing in the
silence, and the gusty wind and rain forcing its way
inside through the pernicious cuts in Ms. Clarice's
steel armor.

My in-laws are silent.

My girl is silent.

Ms. Clarice is silent.

I am silent.

The other car is silent as a Christmas Carrol.
Not even the radiator whispers in the lamenting
rain. The powder blue Corvette is rammed deeply
into Ms. Clarice and folded like an accordion from
the headlights to the windshield. The crash caused
both cars to spin around at least three or four
times before slamming into the rails. We danced

on the slickery road ballroom style. But now the music has ceased. I cannot hear a peep. The engine is perfectly quiet, not so much as a purr. No longer speeding in our direction at over 65 miles an hour, it is stationary as a painting on the wall. The young, teenage girl drinking and driving the car is silent and still as Leonardo de Vince's Mona Lisa. Her severed, bloody head lay perfectly still upon the dashboard. She has gone into a dark silo, drunken and spiritless. The deceptive elixir lived up to his reputation. Her transition was minuscule and private. Though right in front of her, she didn't see it coming.

WHERE AM I? WHAT IS GOING ON?

Soft, curdling moans, gasps for air, and exasperated coughs are the only indicators that I am alive. I turn my head to the right. A life-size barbie lay unmoving just inches away...

Painfully, I slur, "Jennifer, baby, are you okay. Can you hear me. Is that you? Jennifer." My voice is as elusive as her presence. I can barely see her through my burning, swollen eyes. She's a hazy clump of lifelessness a few inches away from me. We both are fading images on the back seat of that car. So close, yet, a life apart.

"Jennifer…"

The sweet aromatic scent of her perfume softens the pungent odor of burning and lingering trail of fresh blood saturating the air. I inhale deeply. "You smell good, baby. You always smell so good. Can you hear me? Jennifer, baby? Wake up, baby. Here, give me your hand."

I grapple limply in the thick cloud of darkness with the hope of our hands over lapping. I still cannot see her face.

The sun will be rising soon. Inch by inch, I fight to move toward the quiet slumping lump on the seat next to me. *Hold on my love, hold on.* The moisture on the seat next to her is sticky and viscous as the gelatin under my seatbelt and clotting on my hands and fingertips.

Waiting

Enchanted by
the smell of fresh rainwater dripping from
the overhang on the balcony,
My pours are opened wide.
I absorb you.

I look deep into your eyes
And I declare I see your soul,
Holding me.

My fear of love rippled away again
When the little boy who lives around the
corner tossed a rock in the puddle of water
that settled in our driveway. We were
home.

Like two turtle doves, you and me,
Perched on Ms. Marcy's window sill.
Love iridescent we shared,
Quiet, warm and still.

Remembering the daunting winter eve we
dined at Rosali's House of Fine Cuisine,
Not even the wind blew.

Nestled in our private booth, slowly gliding
your fingertips
Across my fingertips,
Slowly upward, then bracing ourselves

We stared into each other's eyes.
While our hands playfully overlapped that
eve.
Your wedding band was warm.

You smiled.
I smiled. You smiled again, and again.

Neither of us took a single bite of food.

You feed me.
You sauté my heart in your passions.
Ooooh, your passions,
Green, and vibrant, and soft, and strong.
Your grip was strong.

Hold me.
Tighter.

A blithely sweetened, robust wine marinade
Passionately pouring over an ancient porous
porcelain potsherd vessel,
That's what you are.
Make me whole.

Enchanted by the smell of fresh rain water
dripping from the overhang, I lean my head
backward, longing to savor you again.

I'm barefoot on the balcony.
Waiting.

We were planning to marry within a year's time. Now, together, side by side, we lay lifelessly upon the seats of the vetted vettura, fighting for every breath.

I DO. BABY, I DO. I LOVE YOU, JENNIFER. I DO...

Barely conscious, her name continues to seep endlessly from my assaying lips.

"Jennifer, Jennifer, baby... Jennifer. My love..." I continue feeling around in the small gooey space on the seat between us. "Jennifer..."

I stretch my neck upward and lean into the car door to peer out the window; the vast image of nothingness sneers. Both sides of the road and the picturesque path before and behind are a shroud of groping darkness. The green winsome trees that were ornaments of hope just hours earlier are bitter and black, clawing at Ms. Clarice Foxtail's feet cajoling her into the summoning manic wells, utterly downing her and her passengers just because. The ground beneath me is amply garnished with deadness. I know it's a sign. A terrible, terrible, sign.

The hours drag on slowly. The soft curdling moans, gasps for air, and exasperated coughs cease. Languishing the suffocating smoke, I scrape through the layer of soot impairing my vision and surmise the blurry mannequin-like images in the front seat are the in-laws.

The sun will be up soon, and someone will see us. Dad is tossed over the steering wheel like a crash dummy. Mom is dormant with her head flung against the passenger window. She rests as beautifully as a rag doll can rest. The front of her delicate dress is torn. Her red, lace tapestry brassiere, filled with her full bosom, is showing. Her seatbelt is still intact. Mom and Dad's silence is the loudest sound in the car.

"Come on, sweetheart. Jennifer..."

MOANING...

"Kevin, babe. Help me. I'm hurt..."

Blood gurgles in her throat. "I'm dying, Kevin. Please help me. Oh God. I'm dying."

"Hold on, baby. I will help you."

"I can't take it out. It's in too deep. Help me, Kevin, please."

Flickering in the stoic star light is a large shard of glass poking through her stomach.

Why, why. Oh God! Why!

"Don't worry, baby. I'm here. I'm right here. You are going to be okay."

"Okay..."

"Great, great. I'll handle it. I'll handle everything. I'm going to get us out of here. And when I do, I am going to marry you, girl. I got you. Don't worry about a thing. I got you, baby. Alright?"

"Kaaaay." MOANING and GRUNTING.

I know I must get out of the car or I will lose her. I see a complete circle of gooey ham slime stiffening around the base of the shard of glass sunken into her stomach. It had the appearance of pie crust covered in gooey cherry filling. Her hands are glued to the shard by the dark red goo. Red goo is still slowly oozing around the tiny cracks of the shard.

"Baby, go get help," she barely whispers. I look out the window once more, but the vehicle wears the heavy downpour and the wooded darkness like a hooded trench coat. It is impossible to see more than a few inches in front of me.

Shocked, shivering, and surmising, I keep telling myself, *this can't be real. This isn't real. This is one of those weird moments when a person has a dream that seems as real as an out-of-body experience. My whole life is ahead of me. God! I HAVE A FIANCE! WHAT IS GOING ON?!!!*

I look toward Jennifer again.

She is peaceful as a piece of warm cherry pie.

Her chest isn't racing up and down.

She isn't whispering my name.

She is quiet as a knife at rest.

32

She, and both her parents are at rest.

They are in repose.

I'm trembling harder now

than I've ever trembled.

I try to move my legs.

They are lodge between the seats.

STUCK...

Am I next?

Is it my turn to be quiet?

***

"Words like doors open with ease, with very, very

little keys, and don't forget the two of these: "I

thank you," or "If you please."

Mom!

I'm cold. Everyone in the car is cold. I stretch
forth my hand and reach for the door handle
preparing to fetch help. My fingers shake as I fight
to grip the cold shimmering handle. The rainwater
has gotten to it. I try again, then again. AND
NOTHING... I try again. Still nothing. Even my legs
do nothing.

I feel like a coward because I am afraid to go for help.

Open the door of the car, Kevin, and follow the smell of the burning rubber.

The hot scent is in my nose; it's close. The factory can't be far from us.

I look up and the charred man is staring at me again. My inners leak. Warm liquid and cream shoot up my back. The seat beneath me has become warm and mushy. I cry. I'm scared.

I WANT MY MOM!

An army of tears trek down my blackened face. When I cry, the charred man cries. When I inhale, he inhales. I frown, he frowns. I scream, he screams. I gnash my teeth, he gnashes his teeth.

STOP MOCKING ME!

I'm not. You're mocking me!

I raise my hands to draw them to my face to wipe away the constant flow of tears. We remove our hands from our faces the exact same time...

Staring harder and in disbelief, I yell at the swollen, disfigured, charred freak in the mirror. I lean forward to get a clearer view in the dim light. So does he. I look at him. He looks at me. He feels sorry for me. I feel sorry for him. I shed a tear, he sheds a tear. I weep. He weeps. I mourn, he mourns.

I cover my eyes.

I remove my hands and he's still looking at me.

"Don't look at me like that!" Our mouths murmur at the same time.

"Who are you?"

"Who are you!"

"Go away!"

"You go away!"

"MOM!"

"MOM!"

My face is a sugar-coated pink covered in a black crust. "No, no, no! Noooooo… Moooom! Mom. Oh, God. Moooom…"

Again, we are one voice, one sound. Music is always better on a high note. Reality finally hit me. I lean in closer once more. He leans in toward me. We turn our heads away at the same time then look again at the same time. I stare in sadness. So does he. My countenance falls. He weeps like a wounded prisoner of war. So do I. He wipes the blackened tears from my eyes. He cries for me and reveals solemnly... You are the freak, the mannequin, the mutant, the monstrosity, the centaur, the mammoth, the werewolf, the savage, the leviathan, lusus naturae, the copycat, the charred man in the mirror. There is no other way for me to say it. He says to me. I say to him... There is no toy factory. No melting plastic. Just me. I am he, and he alone is me. Burned and charred and pink and white and red in the exploding acids. Woe is me. Woe is he. Woe is we. Woefully, it is we.

My music is saturated in the deepest, bluest sorrow.

He reaches out to me. I weep. He touches
me. I weep. He holds me. I push away. Let
me be.

Melancholy.

Downhearted.

Dispirited.

Disconsolate.

Destroyed.

Face to face in the broken mirror he wept
and sang.

My face. Oooh, oooh, my face.

What will the hotties say?

My face... Oooh, oooh, oooh.

I am sick.

Greenish, yellowish bile spurts out over and
over from my silent sulking mouth. Silent tears fall
silently from my silent sorrowing eyes. The silent
operatic berceuse is painfully befitting.

The silent stringed instruments, the
trumpets, the horns, the clarinets, the flutes are all

silent. The silent lulling lure of Beethoven's Moonlight Sonata beguiled me throughly.

We wail deep within.

We wail deep and shallow and hard and soft and passionately and cold as the rain in the night and the wind that whispers the sad sound of death in mine ears.

There is a silent wailing deep within my soul.

WHAT IS GOING ON!

The silent music plays on and on and on...

Mom!

Above my dismal cries cloying in the car... through the bleak bitterness before me in the mirror... and through the startling shock and wave of broken emotions, Thomas A. Dorsey's song scrolls from heaven quelling my disquietness. As I fade in the black of the night, tears streaming down my pink, black, gooey, smut fill, rubber burning, skinless face, his holy, saint-like words soothe my disquieted soul...

__Precious Lord__, take my hand,
Lead me on, let me stand,
I am tired, I am weak, I am worn.
Through the storm, through the night
Lead me on to the light,
Take my hand, precious Lord, Lead me home.

When my way grows drear,
Precious Lord, linger near.
When my life is almost gone,
Hear my cry, hear my call,
Hold my hand lest I fall.
Take my hand, precious Lord,
Lead me home.

When the darkness appears
And the night draws near,
And the day is past and gone,
At the river I stand,
Guide my feet, hold my hand.
Take my hand, precious Lord
Lead me home….

The musical interlude brushes my face like my Mother's hand. Oh, how I long to see my mother's face. Mother was always there.

JESUS, JESUS, JESUS!

✲✲✲

She tapped my hands lightly several times in a row, *"You have got to stop scratching, Kevin. I know it itches, baby, but when you scratch, the condition worsens."*

"But it itches so bad, Mom. It hurts. What did I do to catch the measles, Mom? I don't want them."

"Oh Kevin, my handsome boy. The measles come and go, baby. Being sick is a part of life. It's just a small way people can get character, honey."

"What do you mean, Mom?"

"Measles, son, are a serious infection. If you don't take proper precautions to heal, the infection can become life threatening. Having the measles teaches you how to pay attention to small details, such as scratching, and not take anything for granted. Being sick can teach you how to be disciplined. The infection crawls all over your body, in your face, your hair, your mouth, your arms and legs, your back, everywhere."

"Even my feet?!"

"Yes! Even your feet, Kevin. It doesn't matter how fast you can run, you cannot outrun the measles once they get a hold of your body and infect you."

"I don't want this measles anymore."

"Well, you can't scratch. It goes away if you leave it alone. If you scratch, they multiply, get infected and cause you to become sicker than you are now. Some children have gotten pneumonia and have died, Kevin. Others have gone blind. Do you want to go blind?"

"No. I don't want to be blind. I won't be able to see. I won't be able to see you anymore, or any of my friends. I won't be able to see my dad."

"That's right, baby. That means you must listen to Mom, and stop scratching, okay."

"Okay."

"Good. You will have to exercise discipline despite the discomfort and agitation you feel. Having measles is extremely irritating. But look at it this way: it is an opportunity."

"What kind of opportunity? The opportunity to go blind?!"

"No, Kevin! Watch your mouth, my silly boy. As I have already said, being sick can help discipline your life; even your mouth, kiddo. Some people eat too much, and gain weight to the point that their heart almost stops working. They must lose weight, change their diet and exercise, or they may get sicker and possibly die. So, sickness can help us make needed decisions that we are not strong enough, or willing to make initially. Who knows, Kevin, you may face a life changing decision one day. Discipline will help you through it. Discipline helps you become strong, Kevin. Listen to me, okay."

"Okay..."

"Life always has a problem that will cause discomfort. You will understand when faced with such challenges how something like the measles can help you be prepared when faced with larger challenges in life. Don't complain about challenges.

Don't panic. Learn from your challenges, Kevin. There is always a lesson to learn, child. Learn the lesson. Learn what you must do. Because after all is said and done, THAT'S LIFE. Then suck it up. Understand?"

Mom was always there when I needed her. She nursed me at my bedside until that embittered, high-strung, sappy-faced measles infection dried like a prune.

Suck it up, Kevin. This situation is just a challenge. Stop being a baby. It's time to be a man. Suck it up. Put your game face on and meet the challenge.

A deep sense of peace embraces my chest. A gust of courage strengthens my reins. I inhale deeply, close my eyes, stretch forth my sliced-up hand, reach for the door handle. STILL NOTHING!

"AAAAHHH!"

"AAAAHHH!"

I feel my fists tightening and my jaws clenching. Incalculable expletives began multiplying and swarming around my heated head.

"GRRRRRR! AAAAHHH!"

It's not me. It's not me.

I look at my hands, beneath the smut and blood, I see pink meat and blisters!

"AAAAHHH!"

I turn them over and examine my palms. Cuts are everywhere.

"AAAAHHH!"

I look down at my legs, they are perfectly intact. I try to jiggle them from between the seat.

"AAAAHHH!"

I close my eyes and slowly raise my head...

SUCK IT UP, KEVIN, SUCK IT UP. AFTER ALL IS SAID AND DONE, IT'S JUST LIFE. CHALLENGES COME IN LIFE. SUCK IT UP.

"LIFE? What is life?

"AAAAHHH!"

"AAAAHHH!"

"AAAAAAAAAAHHHHHHHHH!"

Jesus... JESUS!

I open my eyes and stare straight into the mirror.

"AAAAAAAHHHHHH!"

***

"Mr. Washington... Kevin. KEVIN WASHINGTON... Can you hear me?"

I try my best to follow the voice, but it is so far away and murky.

The sweet, sully sound of Beethoven leads me home. Louder and louder, softer and clearer. Cleaner. Nearer... My mouth is frozen, open wide like a can of tomato soup. I exhale and whisper...

I'm here.

I'm over here.

Where are you?

I lean forward and pace myself like a blind man patting the air with incoherent hands. Being careful of every step, I follow the faint sound to a green grassy field; brilliantly fairytale green; there is not a brown blade as far as the eyes can see. The sky renders me speechless, perfectly draped in robin's egg blue so soft and safe. The sun is pineapple sweet, drizzling the right mixture of warmth to the modest, sugar-eyed, inspirational breeze. My heart is roller skating and climbing trees on the reminiscent stroll down memory lane. My mouth opens wide again...

> Willow Mills Amusement Park
>
> Hershey Park
>
> And the Grandfather of them all,
>
> Coney Island

Mom's driving the big yellow school bus looking back at me in the mirror smiling. I'm smiling back at her while digging in my lunch pack to pull out some of the sweet, crispy green grapes she packed for me to eat on the bus ride. She froze them over night so they would be icy cold. I love biting down hard and experiencing the sweet juices burst into my mouth.

Coney Island was the coolest. The Go-carts were my favorite. It was like driving a real car, except you didn't get hurt when crashing into other drivers. I always crashed into my friends the hardest. The only way they could get me was to sneak up from behind. That was so much fun! I would always laugh and call them cowards!

I loved the Cyclone Rollercoaster, with all the dips and curves. I got sensations all the way down to my toes flying through the air so freely that way. My stomach shoveled up to my chest on the long ride down. I loved every rushing moment.

At the Food Gallery, Mom held her stomach and laugh watching me gorge on hotdogs, French fries, popcorn, and as many funnel cakes as I wanted. She never said, "Kev, that's enough. Mom was always the best!"

Swimming in the Atlantic Ocean was an epic culminating finale for an eight-year-old. Upon swimming to shore, I always stopped to build castles on the beach at dusk. I loved the way the

fading sun cascaded upon the moist sand,
reminding me of the golden sunsets I admired on
television; but this was unforgettable.

The long ride home was quiet as class
detention. All of the children and chaperones were
completely exhausted. Nonetheless, Mom still
managed to steal a few gazes through the rearview
mirror and watch me rub my belly ache away with
a big ole satisfied grin on my face! Next summer
was sure to come!

Community Drill Team.

My chore list.

In the living room arm wrestling with my
Aunt Vanessa, who also taught me how to
fight, play chess, dance, swim, and roller
skate.

Going to Karate class.

Playing with my cousins.

Playing with my friends.

Watching Mom and Dad wrestle in the
living room.

"Dad, why do you always let Mom win when you guys wrestle?"

"I don't know, son. That's just what men do."

"Why…"

"We're bigger than girls, champ. So, we let them win."

Dad pats me on the head. "Now scat!"

Playing with girls.

Letting the girls win at marbles.

"Mom, why is Paula bigger than me?"

"She's a big girl. You will catch up soon enough."

Turning Double Dutch for the girls.

Throwing grapes in the girls' mouths.

Letting the girls throw grapes in my mouth

Smiling at the girls.

Winking at the girls.

Laughing at the girls.

Holding hands with the girls.

"Mom! Can I have a girlfriend?"

"Girlfriend! Why do you want a girlfriend?"

Laughing... "I don't know."

"Cuuuuzzz."

"Nooo, sweetheart, you're too young to think about that kind of thing."

Droopy face... "Okay."

Sighing...

Doing my chores.

Eating Captain Crunch cereal and thinking about the girls again.

In the backyard with Uncle Butch while he teaches me to wrestle, play football, and score with the girls.

"Mom, I know why I want a girlfriend now!"

"Why, baby?"

"So I can teach her how to play football!"

Mom laughing loudly.

"The answer is still no, baby." Mom says while chuckling deeply.

"You are way too young. Focus on school."

Sighing again. "Okaaaay!"

Breezing through my homework and
thinking about the girls a lot.
Sitting on the roof in a folding chair.
Jumping from roof to roof with my friends
without falling to our deaths.
Feeling the rush.
Taking my shoes off and running barefoot.
Sitting on the floor in the kitchen with my
foot in Mom's lap while she takes the glass
out of my toe.
"Sweetheart, you are going to get enough
of taking your shoes off outside. I've told
you not to do that. This glass is why."
"I'm sorry, Mom."
Reading The Bible.
Going to Sunday School.
Praying.
Kissing Mom good night.
Peace.
I was eight years old,
About to be nine.

***

"Mr. Washington. We are the rescue squad with the Fire Department. You were in a car accident. Can you hear me? You are trapped in the car. But we are here to help you, buddy. I'm going to slip this blanket through the opening just above your head. I want you to take it and cover yourself completely, alright. Can you do that?"

Fighting to come to my senses, I grab my head with both hands and squeeze with all my might. I drag both my hands down the sides of my face and stop at my chin and wait for my head to stop spinning. I have a migraine. I look to my left, then to my right. I look up front, both passenger and driver's side. My head continues to spin.

"Jennifer, Jennifer! Where are you! Jennifer! Mom! Pops!"

"Calm down, Mr. Washington. Your fiancé is safe. Everyone is safe. We need you to cover yourself with the blanket so that we can get you out of the car. Make sure you cover your entire head and body, alright."

"Safe? What do you mean everyone is safe? This person is not making sense. We're all here trapped inside of this car. I look to my left again. "Jennifer, honey." When I turn I realize Jennifer is not there. I began searching around the car. Had she been projected from her seat out of the window? Was she smashed on the floor beneath me? HOW CAN THIS BE! She was right there! Jennifer! Baby! I had been talking to her the entire time, making sure she was okay. I saw her! She was right there! I saw her! Honey! WHAT IS GOING ON? MOM!

"Sir, I'm telling you she was right there! I shouted! I was sitting right where I am now. She was next to me. Right there. She was wearing the sparkly light up dress, the earrings, the necklace. She was right there. I WAS GONNA MARRY HER!

Mom! Dad! Mom was upfront talking to Pops. They were right there. And, and, and... There was this kid, a pimple faced kid, a teenager, a snotty nose boy. No, no, no, no, no, no. It was a girl. Yeah, a girl. And the wheels and the noise and the lights. She blinded him. He couldn't see. She blinded him. She ran us off the road. And her head, it was right there on the dashboard! It was right there! You must believe me! I'm not crazy. I'm not! I'm not crazy. They were right here! My family was right here! She blinded him! SHE BLINDED HIM!"

"We understand, Mr. Washington. You've had a very rough night. Try not to talk..."

AAAAHHH! AAAAHHH! AAAAHHH!

***

"Words like doors open with ease, with very, very little keys, and don't forget the two of these: "I thank you," or "If you please."

Mom!

***

A lexicon of words was still splashing in and out of my mind.

Jennifer

NFL

Coach

College

Mom

My mom

MOM!

NO! WE'RE GONNA HIT!

Do you want to be saved...?

"Words like doors open with ease, with very, very little keys, and don't forget the two of these: "I thank you," or "If you please."

Mom!

"I was a little boy when you used to quote this to me. I used to love to hear you say it. And when you were done you would always say, "Butterfly kisses."

"I loved when we did butterfly kisses, Mom. Your skin was always soft and warm like biscuits. I miss you, Mom! I would put both my pudgy hands on your gentle face, and you would put your strong, loving hands onto my face very gently. You would bend down and get very close to me. You would always open your mouth and smile before your eyelashes would touch mind. I tried to keep my eyes open so that I could see your lashes blinking so fast. But it tickled! I would blink mine and laugh right along with you!"

***

"Mom, Pops! Wake up! Jennifer is gone! Come on we've got to go find her! Mom! Mom…"

I look toward the front seat. An empty pit stood in my stomach. Mom is gone. A salvo of ambivalence floods my mind. Can this be happening? Is this real? I kept flashing in and out of real time. One moment the sun was shining. The next moment I was trapped in a black vacuum.

Scared, shaking, cold.

I was scared, shaking and cold.

Happy, sad, confused.

I was happy to be alive. Sad that no one else in the car survived. I'm so confused! Somebody please tell me what is going on! Where is everybody!

Ms. Clarice Foxtail was nearly unrecognizable, resembling an old forsaken woman. She was plugged nose down in the embankment of the river, with her hinder and under parts exposed to the elements. Dented, cracked, scraped, and punctured on her slippery, slithering slide down the embankment, she leaves to legacy the ruins of her smooth glossy exterior.

The wind was still blowing roughly, and we were on shaky ground. One wrong move and Ms. Foxtail and all her passengers would be one with the fish. "Why is this happening to me!"

I panic and began banging on the window! Help, help! Somebody help me. They're gone! Help me!

MOM! PLEEEEEEESE...

Scared, shaking, cold.

Reality was really sinking in.

"Lord, please don't let me sink to the bottom of this river and drown."

***

"Aaawww, why does it have to rain…"

I was crying, standing in the window of the third floor of our house. The rain dripped as sadly as my tears. My voice cracked meritoriously candidly to the commemorative chanson.

"I wish I could go outside. I wish I could go outside. Oooh Oh, but it's raining."

Being up so high made me feel like the rain was small. I would watch it fall to the ground and become flat just like the ground.

I would bend the words of the song and break them apart at 'outside' and 'raining' to add melody and a trendy big band feel.

"I wish I could go out-si-i-ide but it's rain-ain-ning."

That was the first song I had ever written. I loved that song. It was pretty good. I felt obligated to write that song. I couldn't betray the sun or our fun. All my loyalty was out there in Sidy Home, where all the neighborhood children gathered to have fun. We played every kind of ball you could think of: football, basketball, baseball, dodge ball, soccer. I loved them all! No one could outplay me in any of the sports. Even at eight years old, people saw championship quality in me and encouraged my parents to push me towards the pros. But I didn't know anything about that. I played for the sheer fun of the game.

I stood in the window wrapped in my super magical costume – a body length cape – which when examined closely, was simply an extra-large white tee-shirt I took from Dad's white clothes drawer when he was taking his Saturday afternoon nap. I also sported a pair of tidy whities that had become tidy beiges, because I had been sporting them the last two and a half days.

I tied the magical cape around my scrawny neck. I made sure the knot was tight enough not to slip apart but roomy enough not to choke. I left my torso bare. It made the magic of the cape seem more real. My mom said I would fill out soon enough and have more muscles than any of my friends and cousins. But from where I stood on the third floor of our flat, the reflection cascading off the window said I was looking pretty good already. My arms may have been scrawny, but they were strong. I could bring in all the groceries by myself in one trip. Mom said I was such a strong boy. She always said I was her big boy!

I held up my arms, flexing as hard as I could trying to make a muscle the way I saw the teenagers do at the park playing baseball. I turned to the left, then the right.

"Hummm." I couldn't understand what was going on. I know I was doing it right. I tried again but the big lump was not gathering in the center of my arms. All I saw was an itty-bitty mosquito bump. Maybe the huge boulder size teenage lumps will show up in another mirror...

"Kevin! Boy, why are you running through this house like a crazed maniac with those dingy drawers on and your father's tee-shirt tied around your neck?"

"The mirrors are broken. I'm trying to find one that works!"

"Kevin, what are you talking about, son?"

"Muscles, Mom! Muscles!"

I continued jetting through the kitchen and into the living room like a super hero. Arms up, straining to keep the little bump in the middle of both my arms inflated. My white magic super cape was flying high in the air behind me!

Mom shook her head and continued preparing dinner. "And stop running before you hurt yourself, kiddo, or break something! And go get in the tub."

The last mirror in the house was also broken. It was a life-size, head to toe mirror right next to the front door.

"Forget that stupid mirror," I said to myself. I took off that dumb super cape. *It's not even magic.*

I retreated upstairs and went to the game room where I played with my brothers. We had lots of fun playing pinball, pool, air hockey, and various board games. We especially enjoy Othello, Monopoly, and Twister. When it rained many of the neighborhood boys would ring the bell asking to go upstairs to our play room. It was lots of fun, but nothing was as fulfilling to me than having my lungs bursting with all that fresh air, listening to the birds chirping, the bees buzzing, and the other insects hissing, squeaking, and creating a concerto of echoes.

"I wish I could go out-si-i-ide but it's rain-ain-ning."

"HELP! HELP! HELP!" I shook the door handle vigorously over and over. "Get me out of here! Help! Get me out of here." Buckets of sweat poured down my face leaving red and smut gray trails on my cheeks and chin. I tried to move my legs, but they were still pinned between the seats.

The rescuers had to employ the help of a piece of heavy machinery, The Jaws of Life, to rip the entire top of the car off to rescue me. As I heard the thick metal roof being torn off the top of the car like a sheet of notebook paper all I could do is pray… and scream louder. HELLLLLLLLLLLLLPPP! HELP! SOMEBODY HELP ME! THEY ARE TRYING TO KILL ME! HELLLLLLLLLLLLLPPP!

Chapter 3

Oblivious

"And you hath he quickened, who were dead in trespasses
and sins; Wherein in time past ye walked according to the
course of this world, according to the prince of the power
of the air, the spirit that now worketh in the children of
disobedience."

Ephesians 2: 1 & 2

Hospital ceilings are high. Especially when
staring up at them lying flat on your back on a
gurney in the middle of the hallway remembering
the night before only in jagged bits and pieces,
amply glazed in a sheet of your own blood, topped

by a thicker layer of personal pain, private agony, and public smut and debris.

Why is it so bright in here?

The light shines infinitely sterile, like my soul is being searched openly and revealed for anyone passing by to behold all my private thoughts. I am ashamed to be so naked.

I squint my eyes, but the light is still too transparent. I close them all the way then relax my face. The headache and tension eases up just a bit.

"Hello, o…, o… o… o…" my voice echoed softly. I didn't have enough strength to bellow like I usually do on the football field.

I was trying to stay optimistic and hope for the best, but I was clueless as Ms. Clarice. I remember a wide blinding light charging at us, screeching wheels hollering at the top of their lungs, and then a crash. I remember the loud BOOM shuttering throughout Ms. Clarice's inside. She wet herself. All her oils and liquids ran out of the cracks in her underparts. Ms. Clarice had no idea of what laid wait up the road for her. Nor did I. Dad spent most of the morning rubbing on Ms. Clarice, telling her how fine she is… how she's been faithful all these years and now it was time to celebrate. He told her that he was going to take her on the ride of her life, a ride filled with twists and turns, hills and valleys, a ride to remember.

I should have stayed on campus like Coach said. Coach told me to stay and I would not listen to him.

I should have listened. I should have listened. Something told me to listen. But I didn't.

Lord I need your help. I need to get my life together with Christ. Jesus save me.

I was afraid to speak to God out loud. I didn't want people to know that I wanted to accept Jesus Christ as my Lord and Savior. Being known as a sanctified little church boy would take away my status of being the man. I did not want to be a square, walking around carrying a bible. I was cool, debonair, smooth, The Chill Factor. They called me

The Wash. I was in the church. But, the church was
definitely not in me.

Why now, God...

Why this...

Why not pick on another guy...

Why do I have to make a choice...?

Why can't I just do my thing...

Live my life the way I want...

I like my life...

I like the ladies...

What's wrong with that...

Why can't I just be me!

Why...

Jesus!

Why...

Why ME!

Bombarded with a slew of whys, I squeeze
my eyes tighter and drown in the never-ending
whirlpool.

Soon, I hear feet dragging and clicking in my
direction. I hear hush-hush voices fluttering in the

air and inhale a loud clashing blend of English Leather Eau de Cologne for men and Nina Ricci L'Air du Temps for women. Odors, both my Mom and Dad wear.

"Let's not bother him, Honey. He's resting. And look at him. He looks miserable..."

"Relax, baby. Let me do my job... Hey son, how do you feel? What happened to you?"

I feel a heavy, solid pound of dough gently lowering onto my shoulder, causing it to flatten against the gurney. I open my eyes just a pinch and observe a foggy, wide, overtly large priest-like, Pillsbury Doughy-like image standing over me resting a huge copy of the King James Bible on top of a protruding fattened, well heaped, rounded belly.

I blink my eyes rapidly three or four times to adjust my focus. His backwards collar is the first thing I see clearly. Then I observe the huge clot of dough he calls a hand numbing my shoulder.

"Are you the clergy of the hospital?" I asked in a panic. "Am I dying."

"No, son. Calm down. I am a man of God, but over my own congregation. I am here with my wife visiting one of our church members…"

"Hello young fella," the lovely lady squeaked. We don't mean to bother you. It's jus…"

"It's okay, madam'. I don't mind," I say with as much kindness as I can push across my afflicted face.

"Why thank you, son. Now, see, honey. I told you he would be glad to have a visitor. Just relax, let me do my job!"

She bows her head and smiles at me again then nods for the priest to continue.

"I do not work for the hospital. I am not their clergy. And as far as I can see, you are not dying either. I saw you out here in this large hallway all by yourself and felt compelled to walk over. Sooo, how are you doing?"

"Not so good, that's for sure. I can tell you that! I was just in a car crash with my family and I don't know how they are doing. When I came through at the scene of the accident, my family was gone. I don't know where they are. The rescuers had to cut me out of the car using the Jaws of Life and I haven't seen them from that time to this. Have you seen them? Have you seen my family? Are they safe? Are they here? I don't know where my family is. I want to see my girl! Jennifer! Where is she? Where is Jennifer!"

"Hey, hey, relax. You're under a lot of pressure, Son. I am sure someone will be right out to help you very soon. Just try to stay calm, alright."

"Sure, I just want to see my family. I'm worried about them. I need to know that they are okay."

"I understand, Son. But know that things will work out in your favor. In the meantime, is it alright for me to pray for you?"

"Yeah, sure, absolutely. I can use a little prayer right now."

Chapter 4

Sunday

"For God so loved the world, that he gave his only begotten Son, that whosoever believeth in him should not perish, but have everlasting life."

John 3:16

FIVE DAYS EARLIER...

I leaned my head back and took it all in.

I heard an old, old story, how a Savior came

from glory (how He gave His life)

How He gave His life on Calvary to save a

wretch like me...

The gospel choir was singing "Victory In Jesus," while the altar call was going forth. My emotions were being pulled in deeply. I could feel the flutters in my throat going all the way down into my stomach.

From a child, my heart was always touched hearing the words of that song. I soaked it up like the people sunbathing on the beach at Coney Island, wondering how someone could love another person so much that they would die for them! Those words were written just for me. I could hear God speaking through those words. He was speaking to me.

> He sought me and He bought me with His redeeming blood (bought me with His blood)
> He loved me 'ere I knew Him and all my love is due Him
> He plunged me to victory beneath the cleansing flood

"Brother Kevin, why don't you go up and be saved? This is a good day for you to be saved, brother. I feel it in my heart. I know you want it too."

The young brother is sitting on my right. I recognize him. He is Deacon Danlionden's son. We are around the same age. But he seems much younger, unfettered and not bogged down with the worries and cares of the world like me. He still seems innocent. His peach fuzz was barely coming through his lil' soft skin. But, I knew he was right. That was a good day for me to be saved. I could feel it in my heart also.

Looking straight ahead, I said, "Nah, not today, brother, but thank you."

I shifted my body to the left, so I did not have to see so much as a glimpse of his glowing do-gooder face.

Trying to instruct me. Get away from me, kid. Who told you to sit on the same pew as me anyway? Look at you, not even old enough to shave. How old are you, like 12? I'm old enough to be your daddy, son. Better recognize...

I knew the saved young man was being led by God. I also knew that I was being a jerk and letting the devil use me.

I heard about His healing, of His cleansing power revealing

How He made the lame to walk again and caused the blind to see

Man, Kev, stop all this crazy stuff. You are Kevin Washington. All the ladies want you... but now you are afraid to stroll up this isle. It's only a few steps. What are you stalling for? You know the young brother is right. Go on up to the altar and be saved...

Man! I'm trippin. I know I need to do this.

What's the problem, then, man? Get yourself up and walk down that isle to that altar. Coach tells you to give him 10 laps and you run like a maniac. Man, it ain't no puzzle. Whatever though.

The strapping young cuss sitting next to me on my right did not allow my foolishness to razzle him. He leaned forward and curved his skinny, muscle less body around so that I could see his clean shaven, sheepish face.

"I understand man, if you don't want to be saved. Most of us go through that phase. I did as well. If nothing else, why don't you at least go up for prayer. Ain't no harm in praying, right?"

For a shorty, you are kind of slick with your tongue, man. That's cool. You got heart too. You standing up to The Chill? I can dig that! But that's enough. Don't take it no further. I don't want to have to break you down right here on this pew. So back off...

And then I cried,

Dear Jesus, come and heal my broken spirit"

I then obeyed His blest command and gained the victory

I nodded at the young man in approval, then turned my body further to the left. I was almost looking at the back of the church.

There was a beautiful comely sister sitting directly behind me. She touched my shoulder and said, "Go on up there, don't hesitate. Today is your day. Go on up..."

I was surrounded by sheep. I turned back around on the pew and sat like I had some sense. The sister was warm and convincing. I leaned forward and rested my elbows on my legs just above my knees and looked down at my raw leather Dingo knee-high boots with my heavily starched, burgundy pinstriped pants neatly stuff in them down to the ankles. I was looking real slick; too slick to be walking down a church isle. I needed to be walking into one of my regular spots with one or two hotties on my left and one or two hotties on my right. The pleats of my pants went all the way around from the front to the back. They were a pair of the very trendy baggy style pants that everyone wanted. I was the only one in the church that day sporting them. I had the body of a Greek god. I was made for those pants. They gave me that

77

Dapper Dan look. When I made a move, each pleat swayed like a wave on the sea. People got dizzy when they saw me coming. Yeah, The Chill Factor is here. But I knew the beautiful sister was right. So was the do-gooder.

Slowly, I pulled the pleated masterpiece out of each leg of my boots and slid them back down the length of my legs over the boots and began pressing the wrinkles out with my hands.

Why am I being drawn to the altar? I don't want to go to the altar, Lord. I am not ready. I got to get out of here. Man!

My heart was beating like I was competing in a drag race. My eyes were blustery because of the mixed emotions. Then I just did it.

I jumped up from my seat and began walking down the aisle. It felt like a pilgrimage into a scary, unknown life. I was afraid.

Lord, I'm scared. I am not ready. I am Teddy P. They call me Joe Wash. Why am I doing this? This is for the birds. It's for do-gooders, not me.

I did not want to take that long journey down that church aisle, but I could not help myself. My legs had a mind of their own and were doing their own thing.

My fitted jacket showed my dynamic physique. My body was chiseled as a sculpture. I was a piece of fine art. All muscle from the neck down. I always get a lot of attention in that jacket because of the way my triceps bulge through the arm sleeves.

All sorts of girls kept coming to mind...

Lee lee, Jelisa, Trina Lynn, Bethany, Fruity, TaTa, Mable, Christina, Coco, Raindrop, Felicia, Selina, Chanel, and a German girl I had a one-night stand with, Fran Hoffman. The hotties!

Lord, I don't know if I can give all that up. I just can't! I looked back to see how far I was from the back door, wondering which was closer, the alter or the exit. It felt like I had been walking all night long. But, I was only two pews away from my original seat.

TWO PEWS! THAT'S ALL! JESUS!

The do-gooder was right there supporting me, smiling and shaking his head in approval, motioning his hands telling me to keep going buddy! Keepa going.

Lord, I can tackle this guy...

Dude! You ain't my Daddy! Leave me alone!

I turned around and sped up my stride toward the altar.

Help me God. I'mma bust on this dude in a minute. What is he, a spokesperson or something! Okay, okay, Lord forgive me. I know this guy is right. But man! Give me a break! I'm going! I know you see me walking up this aisle, do-gooder. You are looking right at me!

The color of my jacket was decent on me, a deep shade of tan, almost the color of camel hair, with cool corresponding burgundy stripes to compliment my burgundy pinstriped pants. The jacket had this super cool pleat in the back, that, when I walked it flapped up and down, highlighting my chiseled backside. The muscles were sculpted just the way the hotties like. Everybody couldn't wear this style of jacket. You had to have the kind of backside that I have to pull it off. I got a kick out of wearing it because the hotties loved it. I could feel it flapping up and down as I got closer to the altar. I knew the girls were squirming on the pews. I took a quick glance on both sides of the aisle. To my surprise and confusion, none of the girls were paying me any mine. Most of them had their heads bowed down in prayer. I felt ashamed of myself for thinking such vain thoughts. But I was Teddy P. Turn out the lights.

I can't give up the flap, Lord. Not the flap. The hotties, my reputation. SEX. Oh my God. I can't do this! I can't do it. I am not ready. Nooo! I put a whole lot of effort into this get up. The jacket, the flap, the pants, the haircut – nobody's line was as precise as mine, the big, full beard, nicely groomed. All of it. It was me. My signature. My calling card. My identity. I set the whole thing off with a gold *pocket watch with a two-tier chain hanging down on the right side, burgundy socks, tan suspenders, and my Karl Lagerfeld cologne. Total equipment $687 smacks, yeah. I can't give that up!* My head was sweating and hurting. *LORD!!!*

> *I heard about a mansion He has built for me in glory*
> *And I heard about the street of gold beyond the crystal sea (beyond the crystal sea)*
> *About the angels singing (the angels are singing) and the old redemption story*
> *Oh and some sweet day I'll sing up there the song of victory*

I was torn like a corner from a page of the Bible or a hymnal book. I knew something was missing in my life, but I tried to continue like everything was everything. But I knew there was a void – that little tiny missing piece… Down on the inside I wanted to say yes. But instead, as I walked down that aisle, I continued reasoning within myself that I am not ready. I am not ready to give my life to God. There was a great aching in my soul. "Yes Lord," was on the tip of my tongue. But who would I be after saying yes? I would be Nobody. No Chill Factor. No Teddy P. No Joe Wash, Nobody. The aching got deeper. It reached inside me, inside my throat and pulled up my most intimate fears.

If I do this, people will know that I am just an average guy. I won't have anything to fall back on; to hide behind. Lord, you are taking my safety net away. Without the sports, the girls won't like me. They just like the image I portray. I can't go back to being nobody, Lord. I just can't.

I was choking up. My throat was quivering and beginning to water. So were my eyes.

I can't! I can't, Lord. I can't do this. I don't smoke, I don't drink. I don't steal. I'm a decent guy.

WHY YOU GOT TO MESS WITH ME NOW!

WHEN EVERYTHING IS GOING GOOD! WHY! I do not want to commit to you! I'm scared. What if I commit and then not be committed? I'll look like a double fool then! And, I will have lost everything!

EVERYTHING! No hotties, no fan club, no hommies. Nothing! That's all I have. That's how I get by. I'm lost without the propaganda. Help me, Lord, help me get a mind to be saved. Right now, I just can't.

***

"Brother Kevin! You made it! Glad to see you today."

"It's good to be here, Pastor."

"Yes, it is. He didn't have to wake you up this morning, Kevin, but he did! He didn't have to start you on your way. But he did! He didn't have to give you a mind to stop by and see us today. Ooooh, but what a Mighty God we serve! How's school, son? Are you keeping your grades up?"

"School is fine. I will be graduating in a few weeks!"

"That's fantastic. God is good to you son! You have so much to be grateful for!"

"You are right, Pastor. And I am grateful for all that he has done."

"That's good son. And, he didn't have to draw you to this altar to be saved. But he did that too! Aaah yes! It's good to have you here. So, are you ready to be saved?"

I dropped my head in shame. "I'm not."

"Not what, son?"

"Not ready, Pastor. I'm not ready to be saved. I don't think I can do it."

The choir started singing an all-time favorite, He's All You Need…

The Lord Is!

The Lord Is!

He's everything.

He's all you need.

He's a shelter in times of storm.

He's a friend when things go wrong.

He's everything.

He's all you need!

"Well son, I can stand here and plead with you all day and night. But I am not. I know you know that God has drawn you to this altar today to be saved. But can you tell me what is holding you back?

"I'm just going through some things, Pastor. I have some personal stuff I've got to work out in my own mind. That's all. But I do know what time it is.

I could feel that familiar lump lodging in my throat again.

Just say yes, Kevin. Stop being a fool. Just say yes. You know you need to do this.

Lord, I know I should be saved today. But I am just not ready. I can't. Please have mercy on me. Have mercy on my soul. Please help me.

"Son, being saved is a choice. As you make your choice and walk away from this opportunity, remember that God loves you and he will not let you take this journey on your own. He will be with you every step of the way to strengthen you and keep you."

"I know Pastor..., I... I...

"I know son. Enough said. God has a way. Well, can I at least pray for you?"

"Yes, Pastor, by all means, pray for me. Pray that the Lord gives me a mind to be saved."

I walked away from that altar feeling relieved that all I did was get prayer. Being saved was not the most pressing concern of mine. Holding on to my prestige was pressing. I was thinking that I was young and had plenty of time to get saved. And I knew that I would eventually get to it. But right then... there were more pressing things I needed to do first. There was money I had to make. Goals I had to reach. I couldn't do any of those things by becoming a church boy. I wanted the hotties and the pride. I wanted to establish myself as one of NFL's sexiest football players. That would boost my ego to the next level. And I was on my way. When I walked into a room, any room, the atmosphere changed. I loved that feeling.

I was cocky.

Unstoppable.

Unbeatable.

Impenetrable.

All eyes were on me.

Teddy P. The Chill. The Wash.

The doors would swing open. I would enter and spin real slow and smooth, like melting chocolate sloping down a hill of vanilla ice-cream. I'd nod at my fans. That was the chill factor sway.

Spin like I was modeling.

Smooth and debonair.

Don't get too close you might get frostbit.

And I have all my teeth.

Licking my lips nice and slow.

Melting the ladies down like a sugar glaze.

Staring at their pretty faces without so much as a blink...

When a girl looked at me, she wanted me. My boys convinced me of that.

"Look at 'em, Kev. They want you, man. They are looking at you like you are two thighs and a drumstick on a plate, man."

"Ya'll trippin. But they are staring kind of hard. Hey, I think ya'll right. Let me get with ya'll later. I'mma go check out some of these hotties..."

THEY WANT ME.

Brown ones,

White ones,

Short ones,

Tall ones,

Small ones,

Fat ones.

Skinny ones.

Mean ones.

Sweet ones.

I didn't discriminate.

Ugly ones,

Pretty ones,

Rich ones,

Poor ones.

Neat ones.

Freaky ones.

It don't matter.

Cuz, when they see me,

All their hearts go pitter patter...

I'm the chill factor.

Now, and fa' eva.

NOT RIGHT NOW, LORD...

Chapter 5

Moments of Truth

"How much better is it to get wisdom than gold! and to get understanding rather to be chosen than silver! The highway of the upright is to depart from evil: he that keepeth his way preserveth his soul. Pride goeth before destruction, and a haughty spirit before a fall."

Proverbs 16:16-18

"Do you know The Lord?"

"Yeee…" I tried to lie, but I couldn't bring myself to say yes. I could barely lift my head from the gurney to look at the preacher.

"Well, I knew him as a child. I don't live for him right now. Not anymore. Sir, I'm a backslider. I grew up in the church. I was out celebrating all my accomplishments. I'm graduating from college in a few weeks."

"Wow! That's great young man! The Lord is good!"

"Yeah, yeah, He is. Thank you. I was also being scouted by several NFL Teams and tested with the Seattle Seahawks. I was assured of a Free Agent Draft Choice per my coach's conversation and combine test results. I'll be going pro right after I graduate."

My whole life is set. Everyone always said I could handle the ball and that they saw that pro quality in me. I've been told this since I was a child. So, I always knew that this is what I would do with my life. Everything is going according to the plan."

"Wow! Impressive, young man."

"Yes. I know. Thank you," I said with just a hint of that Chill Factor pride. I took my hands and folded them behind my head like a pillow as I wallowed painfully in my success. I could feel the football in my hands as I held it in my right and smacked it into my left before pulling it all the way back behind my head, almost parallel with my right ear, then ejecting it and propelling it forward with great force like a cannon and watching it jet through the air like a rocket. My arms are strong, and big, and thick, and black, and full of that pro power. I enjoy making muscles in front of the mirror admiring the big lumps in the middle of my arms.

Muscles, baby! Muscles!

I could see myself dancing all over the field and pointing up at Jennifer in the bleachers, twisting my hips and gyrating like Elvis Presley and James Brown, reminding her of what she has too look forward to after the game. The thought of Jennifer snapped me back into reality.

Where is my family? Why haven't I seen them. I hope they are okay...

"Well, son, all of your accomplishments are just fantastic. They are out of this world. But sometimes our plans are not God's plans. Sometimes, God has other plans for us, regardless of how we want our lives to go. In my line of work, I've seen it so many times."

"Well, if he does, I'll make known his deeds among the people."

"Impressive again, young man. I see you know the scriptures..."

"The scriptures? Why did you say I know the scriptures?"

"Well, because of the scripture you just quoted from the Book of Psalm... 'Make known his deeds among the people...' That's from the book of Psalm."

"Well, oh wow! I certainly did not know that. That's just something that came to my mind. I don't know how, and I don't know why. When you said God has other plans, those words just came to me. I've never heard them before. I've never said them. I've never heard them in church or Sunday School. They just rose up inside me right now and fell out of my mouth. Weird. They are not even my words. I was actually wondering why I said that. Seriously, I really was. I can't explain it. But it ain't no puzzle. I mean, whatever."

THE CALLING:

"Son, those are the words of God. The scripture states in John 7:38, "He that believeth on me, as the scripture hath said, out of his belly shall flow rivers of living water." From this day forth, know that God has called you to bring life to the lifeless. You shall use His Word to heal the brokenhearted, and help the lost and disillusioned find their way back to God."

"Wow! Isn't that something…" I said with a nervous, dreadful, reverent chuckle.

"There's a calling on your life. God is calling you to proclaim the Gospel and he is going to use you in a great and mighty way. He is going to reveal his will to you by and by. I know you don't understand it all right now, but you will."

I was fascinated and locked into a daze as this utterly big, prophetic man spoke purpose and words of life into my spirit. I continued laying prostrate on that gurney in that huge empty hallway looking up toward heaven, with tears streaming down as his words burrowed into my soul.

¹ O give thanks unto the LORD; call upon his name: make known his deeds among the people.

² Sing unto him, sing psalms unto him: talk ye of all his wondrous works.

³ Glory ye in his holy name: let the heart of them rejoice that seek the LORD.

⁴ Seek the LORD, and his strength: seek his face evermore.

This bellowing brother quoted the first five verses of Psalm 105, flawlessly. He had an exuberant, thunderous roar in his voice, like all preachers. He did not stutter or fumble over the words; not one time.

I gave a slight smile while saying to myself, *"I'mma do this one day... I'll be able to quote scripture like that."*

This Bible toting, praying man, made me feel larger, larger than I was a few moments ago. I felt large like a preacher, like that preacher. Man, that guy is big! But whatever. I felt larger than my college degree; larger than being the Combined Test Seattle Seahawks draft pick. All of that seemed small in the presence of this peculiar, all-inclusive man. I felt like my uncle. My mind flashed back to when I was a kid in his basement watching him write all those messages for Sunday morning worship service. He would spend hours and hours just writing. Sometimes, he would write two or three pages, then tear them off, bawl them up, toss them on the floor next to his chair, and start fresh.

"Come over here Kevin, son, get these papers up off the floor for me, and put them in the waste basket over there against the wall. I'd pick them up and straighten them back out. As I read them, the air would leave my lungs. The basement would brighten somehow.

Why did you tear this out, Uncle? This is good. The title was 'What Is Life?' He wrote it in big, all cap letters at the top of the page. Right below it he wrote a scripture. Luke 12:23 The life is more than meat, and the body is more than raiment. And that was it. He ripped it from the tablet and tossed it to the floor with the rest of the throwaways...

I felt like I could float on up to heaven when reading those balls of paper. Sometimes I'd stuff the rumpled pages in my pockets and take them home and read them over and over in the dark with the covers pulled over my head and my little expedition flashlight hoovering over each word.

***

When I get up off this gurney, I am going to do it... I am going to tear off sheets of paper and bawl them up just like my uncle. I won't stop writing until I get it right. I will make known his deeds among the people.

Chapter 6

Left for Dead

None eye pitied thee, to do any of these unto thee, to have compassion upon thee; but thou wast cast out in the open field, to the loathing of thy person, in the day that thou wast born.

Ezekiel 16:5

"So, are you ready…"

"Ready for what? I said in an unsure, baffled tone."

"Prayer. I asked you could I pray for you a moment ago. You said yes."

"Sure, I'm sorry. My mind got lost in a thought just that quick. But I'm ready."

The prayer was short and crisp. Clean as a white face towel, straight from Mom's laundry basket.

"Now, what about your people, son? And this girl you keep raving about?"

"I guess when the nurse on duty comes, I will ask her."

"Or, my wife and I can go find someone to help you, son. We don't want to leave you out here in the hall like this."

Before I could reply, the nurse and a whole team came rushing down the empty corridor. It was three or four of them, moving briskly in my direction.

I looked again and there was my family, walking in my direction as well. I raised up as much as I could, only a few inches, my head and shoulders could barely leave the gurney.

"There they are right there. My family. They are coming this way. Jennifer!" I exclaimed!

The preacher and his wife looked at Jennifer. She continued walking toward me, along with her mom and dad. As they got closer, I called out to her again…

Jennifer! But she did not respond.

I pointed, "Mom, Dad."

They continued moving unapologetically.

The prophet glanced at them, then at me.

Also, unapologetically.

A few feet away, almost face to face, they made a sharp right toward the exit door.

They saw me lying there half-dead

And left.

They left me for dead.

I felt abandoned.

Frustrated.

Rejected.

Alone.

I did not matter to them.

They didn't want me anymore.

They saw the tears in my eyes, yet

They thought me of no value.

Jennifer!

I was worthless to them.

Not even worth a penny.

Jennifer!

I was dirt.

Rubbish.

Filth.

Trash.

Come back.

Jennifer!

Come back.

Weeping like the willow...

Jennifer.

Come back.

Mom.

Dad.

Come back.

Nope.

No.

Nah.

Nay.

Uhuh.

No sirree.

Negative.

Any who.

Absolutely not...

All the planning,

All the bragging,

The future we were building.

They walked by,

And left it all on the gurney.

This changes everything, Kevin.

We did not sign up for this...

This is a matter for your family.

We were glad to take you in,

But you switched up on us.

What's in it for us?

What is life?

Surely, not this.

Now you are a weight.

A ball and chain.

An albatross.

A pit.

A pain.

A bad deal.

A cancelled check.

A mistake.

A forfeit.

A strike.

A tackle.

A slap in the face.

Out of bounds.

A missed field goal.

A Fumble.

A Turnover.

An upset.

A defeat.

A dropped pass.

You are benched.

GAME OVER

Why am I crying like a baby?

MOM!

None of it was real.

They walked out on me and left me like I was a severed leg.

Like I was dead weight.

Like I was dead.

Man, they left me.

Are they coming back?

NOPE!

Man, they just left you here.

But that's yo' family, man.

They comin' back tho', right.

NOPE!

COACH!!!!!!!!!!

"*Listen, Kevin. Where are you heading man?*"

"*I am going out to celebrate with my family, Coach! Your boi is doing big thangs!*"

"*Kevin, I need you on campus tonight!*"

"For what, Coach?"

"I got a scout coming to see you. I need you to be here."

"Man coach! I can't. I promised my girl. Jennifer, is expecting me. All of my equipment is at her house. She set this up two weeks ago. I just got off the phone with her. I told her that I am on my way. She's expecting me to spend the whole day with her. I gotta be there, Coach, by 9am. Pancakes man! Eggs, Grits, Sausage. And I do mean sausage, I said with a devilish smile on my face. Aaaeee, it ain't no puzzle. It's whatever, Coach! I can't break my word to her again. She's not having it this time, Coach. I gotta go."

I guess I was dead to them.

I was just a get rich quick scheme.

Now I am valueless.

A spoiled woman,

A bad ham,

A broken man,

A liability,

A has been,

Washed up,

A bad dream,

A nightmare,

A proverb,

A byword,

Those words kept ringing in my head...

They left me.

They left me.

They left me for dead...

They left me for dead...

And as quickly as they came.

They were gone.

The kind preacher and his wife were gone.

I didn't even see them leave.

Pandemonium fogged the hallway.

Directives were flying from every direction.

Hurry, we've got to get him cleaned up...

I had urinated and lost my bowels multiple

times. Now I understand the warm mushy

feeling crawling up my back at the scene of

the accident.

They left me.

They thought I was dead and left me.

Check his vitals again...

Ask him his name...

We can't move him.

He's dead weight.

Move quickly, people!

Wheel him to a room

and cut his clothes off.

As they cut away my clothes,

the pong of the warm mushy feeling made

its way back into the hallway,

disabling everyone passing by.

The team of professional healthcare providers ruined my high-top Salvatore Ferragamos.

My brown nylon socks,

My Macy's white-collar button-down shirt with the extravagant collar.

My Ralph Lauren Polo lambswool pull-over sweater.

MY EQUIPMENT...

All of it. They ruined it.

They ripped my equipment to shreds.

$475, down to $0, in a few split seconds.

But I'm alive.

Thank God, I'm alive...

Chapter 7

Monday

"To day if ye will hear his voice, harden not your hearts."
Hebrews 4:7f

FOUR DAYS EARLIER...

"Hey Kevin, how are you?"

"Uhhhh, hey baby, what's happening. Uhhhhh, do I know you?"

"You should, we have been in the same psychology class putting up with the Professor's crazy pop quizzes for the last two and a half months."

"You're in Professor Justice's Psy class? I would have remembered you, as pretty as you are. What's your name, baby?"

"Haha. My name's Tracie. And yes, you would remember me, but you are always… busy."

Laughing… "Ooookay. What does busy mean?"

"Well, you have a lot of admirers vying for your attention. And you make sure you please them all. That's a line I'm not willing to stand in. It's a little too long for me."

"Well, today is your lucky day, baby. There's nobody here but you. Is the line short enough for you now? You have my full attention. What can I do to you? Anything you want. The pleasure will be all mine."

"Well, you are doing it right now."

"And what's that."

"Talking to me. I have been waiting for an opportunity to, uhhh, talk… to you."

"Well girl, let me be the first to say, if I had known you wanted to uhhh, talk... to me, we would have talked last night, all night. And we'd still be talking right now. You see, I'm long winded. Once I get started, it's hard for me to stop... uhhh, talking... especially when the conversation is as good as it is right now..."

"Ah ha. Interesting. Soooo, I tell you what. I'm long winded too. Maybe we can talk tonight."

"Yeah, yep. We can do that, baby. I will definitely be in the mood for talking to you tonight."

"You are a funny guy, Kevin. I see you have a delightful, outgoing personality and huge sense of humor. So great! Here's my room number. Somebody wants to know you better..."

She took a pen out of her purse, grabbed my hand and wrote her dorm room number on it. The green ink seemed to glow in the broad daylight as she tattooed the inviting mark onto the palm of my hand. She is definitely a hottie!

I smiled and wiped the beads of sweat that were forming just above my brow.

"Ouuuuuuuuuuwee," is all I could mumble beneath my breath as I watched her walking away, throwing it to the left and throwing it to the right.

Yeah girl, I'm definitely going to see you tonight. And I mean see all of you! Lord, I need a glass of milk, or a heart defibrillator.

"Oooooowee... Lord, that girl is fine."

At the end of the day, I rushed to my dorm to prepare for the long night of communication ahead of me. I went to my locker and pulled out my black button up. The ladies love this one. $123.00. I pulled out a pair of my Calvin Klein jeans. I caught them on sale for $129.99. I topped it off with a pair of my Dingo boots, $250. And was prepared to grab my Calvin Klein jacket on my way out of the door, also on sale, $299. I jumped in the shower and rubbed my body down with a bar of Coast soap. I allowed the lather to sit and foam on my skin a few extra minutes before rinsing. This would ensure the removal of residue from the practice I had earlier. Once lathered, I let the water drip down from my head to my toes. I loved taking showers that way. The steam opened my pores, which allowed my cologne to penetrate deeply into my wet skin. The smell would last all night long. All the hotties love to lay on my chest and breathe all of me in. And I let them. I did my mental checklist, put my tic-tacs in my pocket, along with my protection, and I was off. Total equipment, $771.99. But Tracie is worth it. I can feel it.

***

"Where are you heading, Kevin. Come hang with us."

Some of the ladies were sitting on a bench near the dorm.

"Nah, not tonight ladies. But I wish I could. Give me a raincheck. I've got to take care of something right now. But I'll get back at you, fa' show."

"Girl, he so fine. Look at how he walks. Look at all those muscles."

I looked back. "You ladies know I can still hear you, right?"

"Bye, Kevin."

I smiled.

"Girl, I don't care if he does hear. He still fine. Yeeesss!"

I smiled again.

KNOCKING...

"Well, hello Kevin, I see you didn't stand me up. Thank you. Come in and get comfortable. This is my room."

Excited, and feeling like a man, I used all my Chill Factor swag as I entered into her room. I walked in much further than I needed too, because I wanted her to see me from behind. She needed to get a good look at all of me. I took my jacket off to give her a better view then spun around slowly, like I did on the dance floor.

116

She chuckled, then turned and locked her room door.

I tossed my jacket on the chair she had sitting underneath her window, licked my lips, then looked down at my equipment to ensure every particle was intact. I gave her the Chill Factor stare down while unbuttoning and extra button on my shirt so she could get a better look at my chest muscles, and to give her a sample of what she had to look forward to. She chuckled again.

Look at her, over there foaming at the mouth, leaning against that door. She wants me. And you can have me, baby, because I am definitely going to have you tonight.

I looked down at my chest and put my hand in my shirt and stroked my chest the way she would be doing in a few minutes. I was still moving in deliberately and stealthily. Slowly, I slid my hand down my oiled body further while not taking my eyes off of her eyes, I grabbed my huge belt buckle. I gave a slight up and down move of the buckle which caused her to look down at my hand and the growing bulge beneath it.

Perfect... I got her! Watch her purr like a kitten soon as I lay that body down. Nah, she's a wild one. She wants this bad. She's feisty like a cat. Yeah, this one is a scratcher. Yeah, she can use my body anyway she wants to use it. Yeah, just remember, The Chill Is Hot!

I continued moving in closer, unbuckling my belt and slowly unzipping my pants. I had reached my destination, face to face with my conquest. I was so close I could almost hear her heart beating faster and faster. She had a look of pure pleasure smeared over her face.

I was so in scoring mode, that I did not realize she had Gospel music playing in the background.

"Wait, is that the Clark Sisters?"

"Yes..."

"The Gospel singers..."

"YES..."

"Ooooh, okay."

I thought that was odd but brushed it off quickly and continued with the agenda she invited me up for. I leaned in to give her a soft, sweet, but passionate kiss on the lips to break her down and get her more comfortable with The Chill. That's when I noticed lying on her neatly made bed to the left of us an open Bible.

That sight interrupted the juicy kiss I had planned for her.

"Wait, wait. What is this? Am I in the right room? Did I talk to you earlier today?"

"Yeeesss. You are in the right room. And yes, you did speak with me earlier..."

Man, this girl is killing my vibe up in here...

"So, tell me why am I here?" I could feel heat rising in my head.

Why is this girl playing gospel music? How are we going to do what I came to do with "He brought the sunshine," playing in the background...

I backed up off of her.

"Okay, okay. Tammy, look."

"My name is Tracie, Kevin. Tracie."

"My bad. I know. TRAAAAACIE. I apologize. But you got my head all messed up. You invited me up here to get busy with me. So, what's up?"

"Excuse me, Mr. Kevin Washington, Joe Wash, The Chill Factor, Don't Get Too Close, Because You Might Get Frostbitten... I invited you up here so that we could talk."

"No, no, noooo. That's not what you said. You said you wanted to get to know me better."

"Nooo, wrong again, Kevin. You've got to learn to listen. You were too busy talking and not listening. What I said was, "Somebody" wants to get to know you better. That's what I said. I'm here merely to introduce you."

"Well, where is she? Is she in the bathroom hiding out, trying to make a grand entrance? I mean, she ain't got to do all that. Tell her to come on out."

"There's no one in the restroom, Kevin."

Tracie was smiling, almost laughing.

This girl thinks this is a joke. Well, this ain't no joke. She's playing with my emotions. Got me all agitated...

I calmed myself down.

"Well, where is she, Tracie, if you don't mind me asking."

"Not at all. Look right there."

Tracie pointed to her bed.

"She's under your bed?"

"Noooooo.... Look again."

"Tracie, this is crazy. You are pointing at your bed and there is no girl on your bed. Now, if you want, you can hop on over there and lay back. I wouldn't mind getting to know you better. That's what I came up here for anyway."

"Look again, Kevin, Tracie said sweetly and calmly."

"Uuuugggg. Wow! Whatever you say, lady."

I looked again.

"I don't see anyone. The only thing I see on your bed is the Bible."

Oh my God. The Bible. Then it hit me…

"Exactly. Kevin, do you know the Lord?"

BLIND STARE. I STARED BLINDLY AND BLANKLY AT THE EMPTY BED WITH THE OPEN BIBLE…

"Seriously, do you know Jesus Christ?"

Shame was written all over my face.

"Uuummm, of course I do. I grew up in the church. Wooooow! Maaaaan! This is crazy!"

LAUGHING NERVOUSLY…

"How did I miss this? How could I have been so far in left field?"

"Yes Kevin, this is why I invited you up to my room. God dealt with me last week and told me to speak to you about giving your life to him. He also showed me how to get to you. This is it. You would not give me the time of day any other way. I had been trying to get to you for weeks. It felt urgent and this is the only route I could think of to get your attention. It's time, Kevin."

"Time for what, Trina?"

"Time for you to be saved, Kevin. Jesus Christ wants to get to know you. And the name's still Tracie..."

"Ooooooowee, this is a lot. I need to get out of here."

"Are you sure?"

"Yes, I'm sure. Thank you for inviting me. I appreciate what you were trying to do. But, I've got to go."

Tracie unlocked her room door. I grabbed my jacket and walked out.

I was perplexed by the exchange, but I was also angry. Those same girls were still sitting on that same bench, flirting with all the guys as they walked by.

"Hey Kevin. Back so soon? We usually don't see you for another five or six hours. Come on over here. Let us take you through the night, baby."

I couldn't look back. I sped to my dorm room, snatched off my gear, and ran another shower. I needed to cool off. I was heated.

"This girl set me up. I'm the one with all the moves. I'm Teddy P. Not her!"

The water in the shower was extra hot. I let it burn.

"Why would she do that to me! What's wrong with that crazy girl!"

As the water began to cool, I played back the day. She was not dressed like all the other girls. She had on a modest dress below her knees, both encounters. She had no cleavage showing. She had none of the usual signs that sends the message that she is displaying the goods. How did I miss that? Even her so-called flirting back with me was contrived in my mind. She was making fun of me. She was never interested in The Chill Factor. She was only interested in my soul.

I got out of the shower and sat on the edge of the bed and could not move. I laid back and was

there for the rest of the night. All I could see was
that Bible lying on her bed.

Chapter 8

Tuesday

"For what shall it profit a man, if he shall gain the whole world, and lose his own soul?"
Mark 8:36

THREE DAYS EARLIER...

In 1978, during the Spring Break, we had a
fire in our home and lost all our personal
belongings. After the police, fire department, and
the smoke cleared, we had an opportunity to look
inside the house to gather what valuables
remained. As expected, nothing remained. The
living room furniture burned down to the metal
framing. The dining room table and chairs were

nothing but ashes. The kitchen appliances, all the beds, all the curtains, the blinds, and everything in the bathroom was left in ruins. All of my good stuff in the game room, my air hockey, my pool table, my chest table, all my board games, gone. My jersey, all of my clothes, gone... Everything burned to rubble, except for one thing... The Family Bible. The Family Bible was still immaculate. It was sitting in the middle of the living room floor unscathed. Not so much as the smell of smoke was in the pages. There was no soot anywhere on it. Not even the residue of ashes rested upon the cover. The sight of it was beautiful. It was mind-blowing and mind-boggling. God was definitely speaking to me.

I woke up Tuesday morning and sat up straight in the bed like I had been struck by a bolt of white lightening. The Family Bible was on my mind.

Chapter 9

Wednesday

"Come unto me, all ye that labour and are heavy laden, and I will give you rest. Take my yoke upon you, and learn of me; for I am meek and lowly in heart: and ye shall find rest unto your souls. For my yoke is easy, and my burden is light."

Matthew 11:28-30

TWO DAYS EARLIER...

Man, I need to find a hottie to get with.

That girl has got my head all messed up. Let me go over to the cafeteria where I know I can get into something.

Kevin, man, you know you are wrong. God just dealt with you last night. You can't do this!

I passed by a huge pane of glass and saw my reflection. I wasn't looking too fly. I was casual and disheveled. I had on a sweat suit and some gym shoes. Total equipment $89. The night before was rough. I was still being plagued by all that happened in Tracie's room. That girl was like a good serpent with conscious fangs. She bit me and serum was trying to cure me of my sinful ways.

I was facing an inward battle. I was tired of my lifestyle but couldn't seem to stop on my own. I needed to stop but, I did not want to stop.

THEM GIRLS...

LORD, THEM GIRLS...

OH GOD THEY ARE SO FINE. JESUS!

THESE HOTTIES!

MY LORD!

Lord, you've got to help me. These girls have me all messed up. Tracie was wrong for that. For what she did. I mean, I know she was right, but she was wrong, too. How is she going to call me up into her room on the pretense of getting busy with me?

She knows what kind of man I am.

She knows what I do. What was she

thinking?

What was she thinking that I was thinking?

The same thing as every other woman... she

wanted me.

Every woman knows you can't play with a

man like me, like that! She's got me mixed up with

some of these other guys that I hang with. I'm

Kevin Wash....

Before I could finish forming the thought in

my mind, four fine hotties walked up to me.

"Hey Kevin."

It took me a few seconds to connect my

thoughts with real time because I was still locked in

the conversation I was having within my heart.

I smiled when I saw the luscious,

mouthwatering, fine appetizers standing before

me. I was wondering which one would be

breakfast, which one would be lunch, and which

one would be dinner. The extra hottie would

automatically be my mid-day snack. Aaaeee, my appetite was hearty. I could eat.

"Ladies, ladies, ladies! Mmmmm! Good morning ladies!"

The thickest, finest, tallest, most curvy one stepped forward and got right in my face. She was certainly more than an entrée. She was definitely a plate of those down home, southern style, cook them like my Grandma cook them harmony grits, oven fried, country cured, hickory smoke slab bacon – the kind you have to slice yourself; along with four, maybe five, delicious, fluffy scrambled eggs stirred up with a fork in a huge mixing bowl with the shredded sharp cheddar cheese and heavy cream in them, none of that 2%, and lightly salted before you even pour them in the pan; finished off with a side of those extra-large pancakes, the kind where one pancake takes up the whole, entire pan. And if you don't flip it right it splatters all over the stove. Yeah, she was that kind of meal. With a fresh fruit salad packed to go.

"This is not a chance greeting, Kevin. We've been looking for you?"

"Looking for me," I said with a curious grin on my face. "Well, it's not unusual for beautiful ladies like yourselves to be looking for me. As you can see…"

I gave them the full fledge, slow motion Chill Factor spin, keeping my eyes on them the entire time.

"Here I am."

"Cut the crap, Kevin, we are not here for all that mess."

"Well, why are you here, ladies? What can I do to you this morning?"

"We're just here to let you know that the swelling will go down."

I was puzzled.

"Swelling? What swelling?"

"This swelling."

POW!

She aimed directly for my eye. But I was quick, I leaned back, and she missed. Not even the wind from her fist touched my face. She settled for a gut check.

POW!

She had them hands, though. I had to give her that.

Then she put her hand on her hip and let me have it.

"You had me in my room waiting for you all night… I'm not to be played with, Kevin. What? You think all of us are just some little trinkets for you to handle and mistreat? Well, we are not. We are human beings, Kevin. We have feelings. Sitting up there lying to us – The Chill Factor is going to bring the heat, baby… Remember those words! Well, you are cold as ice. Forget you!"

Wow, she was right. I forgot all about her. I had set that up earlier the day before I spoke to Tracie.

Man, Kevin. You are getting sloppy. You've got to get your game together because you are slipping.

"Look, I apologize. It totally slipped my mind. I would never intentionally stand you up. I mean, look at you."

POW!

Another gut check.

"Listen, girl. Stop swinging at me. I have apologized. If it's anything to you, I can get with you tonight. I told you, I would never stand you up intentionally!

POW!

POW!

Another gut check.

And another.

"But you did. Don't think I didn't hear about you coming out of that church girl's room. We heard how you didn't get nothing! She set your phony butt up. That's what you get."

"PHONY. No way, baby, never that. Come up to my room and you judge for yourself. And for your information, she didn't set me up. I was tired, so I left. I went to bed early last night. But like I said, the offer's still open."

"Man, shut up. Don't nobody want your phony butt no more. Uuuggh. Get out of my face, Kevin. I can't stand you! You make me sick!"

They turned and began walking off.

"Fine, it ain't no puzzle. I mean, aaaeee, whatever. And by the way, you hit like a girl." She turned back around. I took off running to get away from her fury, laughing all the way.

I went on about my business and headed to the cafeteria. Ironically, the cafeteria staff had prepared a nice spread of grits, bacon, and eggs. However, I could not enjoy the meal. I sat there just staring at the plate and thinking that these girls are going to be the death of me.

***

"Kevin. Kevin! I know you hear me calling you."

I couldn't remember her real name. Everyone called her Baby X, because she was radical and reminded us of Brother Malcolm X. She had lots of mouth, but she was smart, too. She could shut anybody down on the debate team. But I liked her for what she was to me – A hottie. That's it. That's all. She was a cute face, big hips and soft thighs. She wanted more, like all the rest of the hotties, but I didn't have it in me. A few months ago, I stood her up too, like I did to the other hotties at times. The next evening, Baby X came for me in the cafeteria.

If a hottie was looking for me and could not find me, all she had to do was hang around the cafeteria. I had a good meal plan. I was going to eat.

I knew it was her stirring all that ruckus in the line. She always made a grand entrance when she had something troubling on her mind. I didn't *turnaround to look at her. But I could feel her big round eyes burning a hole in the back of my head, straight through my afro. Soon to follow was her loud clacking shoes heading toward my table.*

My guys start laughing and mumbling beneath their breath.

"Here she comes, mane. Get ready."

"Kevin! I know you hear me!"

"Gone, girl. Gone somewhere with all that noise."

"Nah, negro! You stood me up! You didn't have to do that. Why do you have to do a sista like that! I didn't have nothing but love for you. A black man gets a little popularity under his belt and he thinks he's Billy D. Williams. What have I ever done to you, Kevin, except be nice, and entertain all your stupid BS? What! And you treat me like I ain't nothing. You've got the wrong one, Kevin! Why do you have to be like that? You stood me up." Then she muffed me upside my head.

My guys were laughing.

"Listen, baby, I'm sorry for standing you up, okay. Look, I apologize. It totally slipped my mind. I would never intentionally stand you up. I mean, look at you."

"Negro, please. You tell that crap to all the girls. Don't think I don't know what kind of BS crap you are on. If you didn't want to come, you should have said so. I can handle that. But I rearranged my whole night for you. You were supposed to be my date. It was my birthday. And I didn't have a date, Kevin! You ruined it!"

I looked at my guys. They were waiting for my comeback line. I had nothing. Baby X shut The Wash down.

"Look, I have apologized. If it's anything to you, I can get with you tonight. I told you, I would never stand you up intentionally!"

"Tonight, no, baby. There is no tonight. The only thing between us is Never Again, Punk!!! I just came here to say happy birthday to me! Something you should have said last night."

One of her girls was holding a big platter of mashed potatoes, gravy, pudding, and whipped cream. That was her special rendition of her birthday cake made just for me. She grabbed it from her girl and dumped it right on top of my head. Then, hit me with the platter.

THE ENTIRE CAFETERIA BECAME SILENT. ALL EYES WERE ON THE WASH.

She stood there staring at me, huffing and puffing with tears in her eyes. I looked at my guys, pulled off my sweater, used it to wipe away the mashed potatoes and gravy from my hair and face. Then went back to eating my meal.

"Oooooh, I can't stand your cocky butt. Your day is coming, you smug punk!"

She and her girls stormed off.

We laughed and continued eating and making plans for the evening.

***

Hottie One

Hottie Two

Hottie Three

Hottie Four

Sitting at the table

Near the door

Then walks in

One more

Hottie Five.

I was losing the game. As usual, my guys were sitting back in awe, laughing, waiting to see how I would worm out of this jam.

It was the tightest jam yet. Even with strategic, careful planning, the odds were not in my favor, that by chance meeting I would end up in the cafeteria sitting at a table with all five girls that I had been lying too, telling each of them that they are the only girl that I was seeing, besides Jennifer, my fiancé. I made them all promise to keep the relationship secret because of that reason. I explained that they could enjoy me, but I had to keep my relationship with Jennifer intact. They understood. They were all aware that it could be nothing more than what it already was. They were also warned that if word got out that I was seeing them, I would lie and deny it all, and I would cut off all their Chill Factor, Teddy P, turn off the lights benefits. All complied willingly. **EXCEPT BIJON…**

Chapter 10

Thursday

"But king Solomon loved many strange women, together with the daughter of Pharaoh, women of the Moabites, Ammonites, Edomite's, Zidonians, and Hittites: Of the nations concerning which the LORD said unto the children of Israel, Ye shall not go in to them, neither shall they come in unto you: for surely they will turn away your heart after their gods: Solomon clave unto these in love."

1st Kings 11:1-2

ONE DAY EARLIER...

"Bijon, stop all that noise. You are always fussing at me, girl, and complicating things. I'm a simple guy. I don't need all of that noise. And besides, I know you did not walk all the way across this hot campus in those tall high heel shoes just to fuss at me. I can think of a few things far more pleasing that you could be doing with that pretty little mouth of yours, instead of fussing at me. Now, get over here with your fine self. Girl, I don't know what to do with you. You a trip, baby. But it's cool. You better be glad you are so fine. Mmmmm. Now hush, and give me what you came to give me." She smiled...

"Yeaaaah..."

Bijon was a spicy little hottie from Trinidad but her name was an exotic Haitian name. With heels on, she stood only 4'4" tall, and weight less than 95 pounds. But her presence was larger than any other hottie on campus. Her accent was strong. Her voice was sultry and satiny, but her words could cut clean through the white meat of any guy. When she read you, or told you about yourself, she dotted every "I", and crossed every "T". Her argument was precise, poignant, and proverbial.

She drove me mad. I looked forward to spending time with Bijon.

But no matter how much time I gave Bijon, she always sucked more out of me. Much of our time together was spent debating about why she should be the only side hottie. All that extra heat and emotions added to the excitement between the sheets. When I'd finally give in and let her win the argument, it was only because I was ready for her to pour all of that Trini passion onto The Wash. I let her spiciness drip from my head to my hips, to my thighs to my toes. Her specialty was my hip and thigh area. She got no complaints from me...

"Bijon, what makes you think I am seeing other girls. This campus is too small for all that madness. I do not have time for that. Why are you bothering me, girl? We should be getting busy. But you are too busy conjuring up mess. What do you want to do? Fight me, or mount me. Do you think I am crazy enough to see any other girl beside you?

Can't you tell that you are the only one for me. And you are more than I can handle as it is."

"Fust, of ole, Kavone.

Ooou do yah tank ya taklin' to, aye?

Me no fole.

I cum insye der tunite,

Pull your sac.

Cote yah bolls oph.

Yah estipid moun fou.

Egare.

Bijon turned me on like no one else. She was my fantasy. She was thick, petite, and pretty as a Moroccan porcelain doll. She was black as a chocolate cake and just as sweet when she wasn't coming at me from every angle. She was sizzling hot and pleased me well. But she was a death trap.

I don't know how she found out that I was seeing the other girls. None of the other girls knew about each other. But Bijon knew. Bijon was observant and obsessive. She was green with envy of them all. I think she was a detective in another life or country, or something. It was all or nothing with her, in spite of the rules of engagement. Bijon broke all the rules. Still, I couldn't let her go. She turned me on like the school sprinkler system.

Bijon knew lots of things about me. She knew the schedules of each appointment I had with the other girls. And she threatened to use that information against me. How did she know these things?

HOW...

BIJON WAS PSYCHIC.

SHE WAS A WITCH.

A STALKER.

NOSY.

A SEER.

CLAIRVOYANT.

SECOND-SIGHTED.

CRAZY.

That's it.

BIJON WAS CRAZY.

And I was crazy to keep her in the rotation.

But I was caught up. The allure kept pulling me deeper and deeper into her web.

The excitement.

The unexpected visits.

The accent.

The slaps to my face.

The quick, unexpected, sexy slaps to my face.

Her perfume.

Her natural sent.

Her strong thighs.

Her strong calves.

Her soft skin.

Her plump breasts.

Her soft, juicy lips.

The scratches on my back, knowing that Jennifer might see them.

I was crazy with lust.

And the way she smiled after she put me in a vulnerable position. Bijon would rip my shirts off. The buttons would fly in every direction. Bijon was strong to be so petite. And of course, the intimacy was crazy. Bijon liked me blindfolded. I thought that was a little strange, but I went for it. As a matter of fact, I went for everything she introduced to me. I could almost believe that she put a voodoo doll in the bed with us, because after fooling around with her just one time, I was hooked. Lots of girls wanted me, and they had me. But I wanted Bijon. And she took advantage of that.

Bijon appeared at my room often right before another girl's schedule. She made regular unscheduled conjugal visits and would be angered when I would not let her in my room.

"Go away, Bijon. You are not getting in here. Go away."

"I goin noware. I go en yah rume."

"Bijon. Stop it. You know I have someone scheduled to be here in fifteen minutes."

"I NO DIS, KAVONE."

"HOW YOU NO DIS, BIJON. HOW YOU NO DIS? I DON'T KNOW HOW YOU KNOW. BUT IT'S GOT TO STOP!"

"I steel goin noware. I go en yah rume. Opin et. Nown, Kavone. Opin et."

"You are insane. This is absurd. You've got to stop doing this, Bijon. Go away, Bijon, or, I will cut you off, straight up. Then you won't be getting anything. Back off."

"I note du no ting. I note bake oph. I go en yah rume. Opin et. Nown, Kavone. Opin et."

"Listen here, girl. You know our agreement. You are making too much noise, Bijon. You've got to calm all that down. Take this foolishness somewhere else. Go find another guy to harass. Why are you bothering me? Go harass someone that makes you happy, Bijon. I am obviously not that guy!"

Bijon loved to showcase her hot Trini temper.

"Ooou do yah tank ya taklin' to, aye?

Me no fole, Kavone.

I cum in der tunite,

Pull your sac ard.

Cote yah bolls opin like coconut.

Brag bout yah big tohty den.

Yah ear me.

Yah estipid moun fou.

Egare.

"Whatever, Bijon. But you are not getting in here tonight. So, take your hot temper and non-English talking tailbone back down the hallway somewhere.

She stormed off sputtering all sorts of madness about how she was going to cut my balls off. I was seriously considering letting her go, but she was feisty. I liked that. But the more I entertained her jealous rants, the more out of control she became.

Everything came to a head when the football team was preparing for our homecoming game. The entire campus was in celebration mode.

There was lots of traffic coming in and out of my room. Bijon was a part of that traffic. She became heated because so many girls were dropping by my room. She wanted me all to herself, but it was open season. Both girls and guys were coming to wish me and the team good luck. But she did not care.

"Kavone, push des peopo frome heea. Keep only me, you, and your toto."

I ignored Bijon. I had traffic in and out all night. She ended up storming away with rocks in her jaws.

The following day, when everyone was at the game, Bijon managed to get into my dorm room. She trashed it. She cut up all my equipment, poured motor oil over them, and burned some of them in the shower. Then she went through my book sack and destroyed all my assignments. It was the end of the semester and I had completed all my term papers. Word quickly spread all across campus, which worked in my favor because I received extensions on my papers without penalties.

Finally, I truly realized that the girl was nuts! I didn't bother to confront her because she was depending on the confrontation. All that fighting and arguing was a turn on to her. She loved the makeup sex. So, instead of confronting her, I reported the incident but did not press charges. I replaced the equipment she destroyed, and went on about my business. Total equipment costs, $15,000. But it was that incident that broke the Bijon spell that she had on me. I was done with her. I knew it was time for me to rethink the way I was living. One of those girls were going to eventually do me great harm. I knew it.

The dream of success that I wanted to build was starting to suffer. I was getting sloppy. I was controlled by erotica. I wanted to stop but erotica had her hands on me. My body was tired, but the alluring urges cajoled me relentlessly. I had to appease the urge. I was ashamed of the urge and some of the things I did to appease the urge, but I had the "I can't help its." I almost blew my engagement with Jennifer on several occasions by standing her up, forgetting commitments, and just outright lying to her so that I could imbibe in indecent decadence. Jennifer was getting fed up, but I still couldn't stop.

My dorm room had become a revolving door, and not for tutoring.

I was the campus whore.

A trick.

A sleazebag.

A John.

I was nothing more than a John.

A piece of meat.

Fellatio.

I was a hand job.

A blow job.

A wank.

A striptease.

A sex act.

I WAS HIPS AND THIGHS.

No better than the whores that laid with

me.

Lord, I'm so tired of going back and forth to

the clinic.

Drip.

Drip.

Pus.

Burn.

Shot.

All these hotties are burning me.

And I am burning them.

But I still can't stop.

It feels good.

I feel bad.

It hurts.

I'm hurting.

I'm raw.

I'm bound.

I'm caught.

What is your name.

Incubus.

What do you want?

Have you not read in the scriptures?

3 There is no soundness in my flesh because of thine anger; neither is there any rest in my bones because of my sin.

4 For mine iniquities are gone over mine head: as an heavy burden they are too heavy for me.

5 My wounds stink and are corrupt because of my foolishness.

6 I am troubled; I am bowed down greatly; I go mourning all the day long.

7 For my loins are filled with a loathsome disease: and there is no soundness in my flesh.

8 I am feeble and sore broken: **Psalm 38:3-8a**

I craved more.

Jerk.

I am a perv.

Jerk.

A prop.

Jerk.

A tool.

Jerk.

A set of testicles.

Jerk. Jerk.

A joke.

Jerk.

A toy.

Jerk. Jerk. Jerk.

I was a sex toy.

Bijon saw through me.

She made me weak and vulnerable.

She knew the truth about me.

She mocked me.

Laughed at me.

Reduced me.

She knew what I really was.

An apparatus.

A dildo.

A fetish.

A broken-down piece of equipment.

A Sadist.

A sad, sad, Sadist.

A freak.

A poseur.

An imposter.

A liar.

I lied to them.

They lied to me.

I lied to myself.

"Mmmm. Lolitha, baby."

"Wait a minute. Hold up! WHO IN HERE NAME Lolitha!"

Oooh God, I done called this girl the wrong name.

"Girl, you know I am just playing with you. What do you want me to do?"

"Faster," is all she had to say.

"Go faster."

"Harder."

"No, no, no. Don't stop, baby. We are just starting. Keep going... Why did you stop, Kevin? Where did you go?"

"Just give me a minute. I'll be ready for round two in a minute."

"What are you talking about? Round two. You can't even finish round one. Is it back yet? I know you want more."

"Not yet, baby. Just give me a few more minutes."

"What do you need all these minutes for? We just started? My session is going to be over. What's wrong with you, Kevin? Why isn't it working?"

"Come on girl, it ain't that. I told you. I just need a few minutes."

"Man, get off of me. I'm not giving you crap. All that bragging you do. You can't do nothing! You have lost it, Kevin. I'm telling

you, you have lost it."

I was washed up.

Drip...

Drip...

Pus...

Burn...

Shot...

Hottie Number Four...

Go Faster, Kevin.

I can't.

Drip...

Drip...

Pus...

Burn...

Shot...

I was a fast-moving, dripping, burning fool

That could not control the zipper on his

pants.

Whores pulled it up.

Whores pulled it down.

I was dirty a lot.

I had an odor a lot.

I burned a lot.

I bled a lot.

I cried a lot.

I faked a lot.

Hottie Number Two...

"Come on girl, just give me a minute. You know how you can work a brother. Touch me, rub me. You know what to do. Work your magic."

"Work my magic. Man please... We've been here only five minutes. You are supposed to be working me!?"

"Just relax, girl. Rub me. Make me come out and play."

"Play with what? Ain't nothing there. Man, move. I got to go. GET OFF ME.

Hottie One,

Hottie Two,

Hottie Three,

Hottie Four,

There's only one more.

"IS THIS IT. YOU CAN'T BE SERIOUS. GET
OUT OF MY WAY, KEVIN! BOY GONE
SOMEWHERE! YOU SUCK!"

I faked a lot.

"Dudes! What's up? It's Teddy P! Mane, I
put a hurtin' on the hotties last night."

I was still crying a lot.

And faking a lot.

I was thinking a lot.

Thinking I wanted to change.

Thinking I needed to change.

I was thinking I couldn't change.

I was thinking.

Man! I think I need a hottie.

Any hottie will do.

I was used.

Depreciated.

Banal.

Pointless.

Ashamed.

I was ashamed of myself.

Of who I had become.

Of what I did.

LORD, MAKE IT STOOOOP!

I thought I was in control. But the girls were using me more than I was using them. After a while I had no specific preferences. The rotation was slim to none. If she could lay down or bend down, she was in. The same was true of me. If I could perform, that's all she cared about. I had long lost my good, prime choice girls and they lost Teddy P.

Hottie One

Hottie Two

Weren't so hot

But still, they would do.

A guy stood in line...

I looked around, and said,

"Fool, that's not cool!"

"You are barking up the wrong tree.

You can never be Hottie Three.

Hottie Three

Hottie Four

I wasn't the one she adored.

Hottie Five said I was just a rod and a tool, and a set of hips and thighs…

This new breed of girls was hygienically challenged. But their unkept odor, dirty smelling hair, and foul breath was not a deterrent. I'd turn my face the other way, just like they turned their faces from me, and just focus on the mechanics. I had sunken so low. I was governed by lasciviousness. My labor was hard. It was no longer a pleasure. I was a marionette to an evil force that had no love for me. There was a time I was selective, but now, all she has to do is knock on my door. And plenty of times, I had to hunt for her, whoever she ended up being.

By night on my bed I sought him whom my soul loveth: I sought him, but I found him not. I will rise now, and go about the city in the streets, and in the broad ways I will seek him whom my soul loveth: I sought him, but I found him not.

Song of Solomon 3:1-2

Chapter 11

Friday

"To day if ye will hear his voice, harden not your hearts, as in the provocation."

Hebrews 3:14b-d

THE DAY OF...

"Hey Kevin, how are you. What's up?"

"Hello Tracie, I am doing well. Been keeping busy, tutoring, playing ball, you know, the usual stuff."

"Yeah, the 'USUAL...' stuff. But anyway, as you know, we are having Bible Class tonight, as we do every week. I see you when you pass by us with your head turned, as if you are trying to avoid looking at us."

Laughing lightly... "No, no. That's not it." Laughing a little harder but still trying to be discreet.

"Come on, Kevin. It's obvious. But don't worry. I know it's not personal. I understand how it is when God deals with you and you are not ready to tell Him yes. May I tell you a brief part of my life before I said yes to God?"

"Sure. By all means..."

Tracie pulled her blouse down off of her right shoulder so that I could see her chest and the top of her breast.

"You see this. Four stabs in the shoulder, two in the chest, and two in the breast. Thank God I did not lose my breast. And I really praise God that his aim was off. He was trying to stab me in the heart. He was trying to kill me. God allowed me to squirm and fight myself free and make it to a neighbor's house where they called for help. I was truly blessed, Kevin. God had been dealing with me for months about being saved. But I couldn't see myself living without this man. Little did I know, that God knew if I stayed with this man, I would not be living at all. He was insanely jealous and had assaulted me several times in the past. But I thought I loved him and thought that he would change, so I stayed. When God dealt with me this last time about being saved, I hardened my heart. It wasn't until I found myself heaving for breath, and leaving a trail of life in the form of my own blood behind, that I realized that I could not go on living life that way. It's sad that I had to almost die before I finally did the right thing. All the time God was looking out for me but I could not see it. To make a long story short, I escaped narrowly, nearly being stabbed to death. My live-in boyfriend was convicted of attempted murder and is currently serving a 3-year sentence for his crimes against me."

"Wow! All of that, and only three years, man. I'm really sorry you had to go through that, Tracie. I really am."

I know, Kevin. As I told you in previous conversations, you are a great guy. You are not like these other dudes around here. I've been watching you for a while now. Yeeeessssss, you do your little "Teddy P, The Chill Factor" stuff. But I see through all of that. I've never seen you hit a girl or even curse one out. That speaks volumes. These guys on this campus have no respect for these girls. But don't get me wrong. Some of these girls are pistols. I see them in these guys faces, pushing them and daring them to hit them. Thank God, you have the strength and the character to walk away. But you still need Jesus, Kevin. So why wait? You don't have to be like me and almost lose your life. I still don't have full use of my right side. He tore clean through the cartilage and cracked my bone. I'm in pain to this very day. It was a painful lesson to learn, but I learned it. Come on to Bible Class tonight, Kevin. It's time. Stop running. Just tell God yes. I woke up this morning with you heavily on my mind, and I am inviting you AGAIN. Say yes, Kevin. Say yes. I really feel like you should come. I think it will be good for you."

I'm standing there trying to figure out a way to say "No," nicely.

"Oh yeah, yeah. Thank you for inviting me. But no, I can't. I already have plans. I got a thing with my fiancé. We're celebrating my victories. Goooo Kevin! I even told coach that I won't be on campus tonight. He has a scout coming, but I can't get out of this thing with Jennifer."

"Well, celebrating is one thing, Kevin, and I get that. But walking in the spirit and obeying God is another. When God calls your name, you should be honored. He cares enough to give you an opportunity to live a sinless life. That type of honor should not be ignored. Often, God is sparing our lives and we don't even know it."

"You are telling the truth. I hear you. Just pray for me, Tracie. See, now I am feeling all bad. I just can't let Jennifer down again. It will kill her. I just can't. But I will definitely consider all your words. For now, just pray that God gives me a mind to be saved."

"I always do, Kevin. Just remember that the scriptures say... God loves you and that it is not His will for any to perish but that we all come to repentance and be save. "

"I know. You are right."

Well, if you happen to change your mind, you know where we will be. Same place, same time."

The violent strength of the wind, the coercive rain beating against the submissive ground, the unrelenting darkness dominating the weeping sky, and the arduous weight of the time-honored car conspire with fate and collude with the narrowing two-lane road as the utterly oblivious drunken driver derails the trajectory of my life.

Saturday
The Morning After
Suddenly, I found myself facing a sobering truth.
I should not have gotten in that car...

Chapter 12

The Awakening

Then the eyes of the blind shall be opened, and the ears of
the deaf shall be unstopped. Then shall the lame man leap
as an hart, and the tongue of the dumb sing:

Isaiah 35:5-6a&b

My Way

And now, the end is near

And so I face the final curtain

My friend, I'll say it clear

I'll state my case, of which I'm certain

I've lived a life that's full

I've traveled each and every highway

And more, much more than this

I did it my way

Regrets, I've had a few

But then again, too few to mention

I did what I had to do

And saw it through without exemption

I planned each charted course

Each careful step along the byway

And more, much more than this

I did it my way

Yes, there were times, I'm sure you knew

When I bit off more than I could chew

But through it all, when there was doubt

I ate it up and spit it out

I faced it all and I stood tall

And did it my way

I've loved, I've laughed and cried

I've had my fill, my share of losing

And now, as tears subside

I find it all, all so amusing

To think I did all that

And may I say, not in a shy way

Oh no, no, not me

I did it my way

For what is man, what has he got?

If not himself, then he has naught

To say the things he truly feels

And not the words of one who kneels

The record shows I took the blows

And did it my way

***

SCREAMING INAUDIBLY AT THE TOP OF MY LUNGS... Every available doctor and nurse on the floor flooded fretfully frenzied into my room.

"Mr. Washington, Mr. Washington, we are here! What's going on?! Please, stop yelling and calm down. Talk to us so that we can help you!"

"Help me, nurse! My legs are stinging like knives are being stabbed into them! They are burning. They are on fire!"

HAHAHAHAHAHAHA. "This guy's a hoot," laughed the team of staff members!!!!

"We have another one!" Yelled one of the doctors.

The room went into hysterics! The robust laughter made it seem like they were at a party having the time of their lives.

"It's not funny! Help me!"

HAHAHAHAHAHAHA.

They laughed even harder.

"Mr. Washington. You have got to calm down. You are hallucinating, honey. All of you guys come in here with all those drugs in your system and expect us to be sympathetic to you! Well, HA, HA. WE ARE NOT! You are not what we signed up for; some snotty nose kid that does not know how to control his urges. We have real sick people who really need us. So, you are not priority to us! Accept it, Palie. You've got to deal with it! Because that is just the way it is!

HAHAHAHAHAHAHA.

"Ease up, nurse. He looks a little soft. We don't want to go green by breaking him in too fast. You know the lab wants their meat to be stress free. So, calm him down. Take your time with this one.

"I AM NOT GOING TO CALM DOWN. I DON'T DO DRUGS. I AM AN ATHLETE! WHAT IS WRONG WITH YOU PEOPLE!"

HAHAHAHAHAHAHA.

"You people? Did he just say, "You people?"

"Yes he did, doctor."

HAHAHAHAHAHAHA.

"Ok, son. 'We people,' are going to spell it out for you! Your legs cannot be stinging or burning. Do you know why! OF COURSE, YOU DON'T. YOUR LEGS ARE PARALYZED, SIR. How about that! Is that plain enough for ya, Buddy?"

HAHAHAHAHAHAHA.

"Stop, stop, doctor. Ya killin' me! We are going to give the poor boy a heart attack!"

HAHAHAHAHAHAHA.

"HELP, HELP. SOMEBODY HELP ME!!!"

AAAAHHHHHHH!!!!

"HELP ME! THESE PEOPLE ARE NUTS! THEY ARE QUACKS! GET ME OUT OF HERE!"

AAAAHHHHHHH!!!!

"We are sorry again, son. But there is no one here that can help you. And like we said, it is not possible for you to have feeling in your legs. Those two rusty sticks that you used to hold up the rest of your body... well, they are good for nothing now. You can't run, walk, crawl, jump, dance, or stand. And you certainly can't play sports, Mr. ATHLETE! You are on your way to the lab, Sonny Boy! Off to the dungeon you go with the rest of the lab experiments!

HAHAHAHAHAHAHA.

"Doctor, now it is you that needs to calm down."

HAHAHAHAHAHAHA.

"Look at him, he's about to crap his pants!"

AAAAHHHHHHH!!!!

AAAAHHHHHHH!!!!

"Mr. Washington, please stop yelling! I can't help you if you keep yelling! You are going to force me to stick a sock in your mouth. Now cool it!

AAAAHHHHHHH!!!!

Mr. Washington! You are making it worse. Your pain is not real. It is only in your mind."

AAAAHHHHHHH!!!!

AAAAHHHHHHH!!!!

"Don't tell me it's not real! I feel it! Help me! They are trying to kill me!"

I was on a gurney in the hospital, screaming at the top of my lungs. I arrived in critical condition, so, the medical doctors made an executive decision to operate immediately. I was delirious and incoherent from the anesthesia.

My bed was drenched with sweat. That green and white hospital gown was matted to my wet body. I was shaking uncontrollably, and again covered in urine and warm brown pong. My teeth chattered and gnashed together in intervals, tears parachuted out of my eyes, and inaudible terrors continued leaping from my throat.

AAAAHHHHHHHH!!!!

HEEEEELLLPPPPP!!!

"It's killing me!"

AAAAHHHHHHHH!!!!

"I can't take the pain! I'm dying! Help me..."

AAAAHHHHHHHH!!!!

"This kid is losing his mind, doctor," one of the nurses whispered. "We've got to calm him down. Should I give him the usual treatment?"

"Absolutely! I was thinking the same thing! The usual treatment will work perfectly on him. Well... on second thought, increase his dosage by an additional 15 percent. Look at him. He is delirious as a rabid dog. Let's take this puppy down," the doctor stated with a comedic smile on his face.

All the nurses gathered around my bed and moved slowly toward me. All of them had huge, comedic smiles on their faces as well. The nurse closest to me had a huge pillow in her hand. She fluffed it over and over while slowly moving it toward my face, chuckling and laughing the entire time.

"Everything's going to be just fine, Mr. Washington, Buddy Boy, you will see in just a few minutes. I'm about to put you out of your misery in 5... 4... 3..."

AAAAHHHHHHH!!!!

AAAAHHHHHHH!!!!

THEY ARE TRYING TO KILL ME!!!

AAAAHHHHHHH!!!!

Another nurse held my arm and stuck a needle in it. Immediately, I could feel the cool dazing agent oozing through my veins. Soon, I was under its glassy, numbing spell. I found myself drifting into a deep sleep. I saw myself walking down a long, dark corridor, only wide enough just for me.

"Where am I? What is going on? Why am I here?" Where does this hallway lead?" These questions, and many more just as perplexing, left me pilgrimaging further into the darkness of the corridor. I continued walking seeking to find answers. I could feel the voyage swelling in my chest. I had no fear, no pain, and no hesitation. I felt compelled. The deeper I traveled into the darkness, the more aware I became. Fragments of my childhood, as well as other parts of my life, were present with me, troubling memories that I would not have chosen to relive.

In the vision, I was back at church seeing myself as a little boy sneaking out of church right after Sunday School. I thought I was a clever boy for outsmarting everyone. I was proud of myself for being so clever. But in the vision, my Mom was right there looking at me with disappointment in her eyes. Suddenly, I was a grown man, no longer a little boy being chastened for sneaking out of church and going to play softball with my friends.

"Kevin, I did not raise you this way. I put you through college so that you could earn an honest

living and take care of yourself, and even start a family one day. But I never would have expected you to forget God, and remove Him from your thoughts. You have abandoned every important value I instilled in you. You are lying, taking advantage of others, and mistreating women... I did not expose you to any of those things. To the contrary, I taught you against them. But I had to allow you to choose your own path in life. But look where that path has gotten you. Are you proud of your choices, son? Are you proud of the man, the person, the individual, that you have become? Before I could answer, Mom was gone. She pivoted on her aging, wooden cane and slowly disappeared in the distance with her long, silver hair hanging in her face and her declining back prominently slumping over. I could hear her crumbling, pining voice fading in the distance, "You are so much more... so much better than this. Go back to your roots, Kevin. Find yourself again, find your purpose."

I was left standing in awe, with my head hanging in shame and my hands groping my chest, holding my breath, pondering decisions I made from the time I was a young child, only 10 years old to now, a grown man, well established and set in vile, selfish ways, suited for my own personal happiness, with no regard for the feelings or interest of others.

HOW DID I GO WRONG?!

MOM!

Mom was gone. I continued standing with my head cast down by defeat. My heart felt sick, green with regret. I needed to regurgitate the life that I had lived... the decisions I had made... the man I had become. It killed my mother. Now, it is killing me. I am dying from the poisonous arrows of self-condemnation.

The visions continued. There was a long, endless line of old battered women standing before me in the corridor. It was obvious that life was hard, harsh, embittered, and unkind to them all.

Their spirits were sullied. But it was still something familiar about them all, but I couldn't quite figure it out. All of them were crying. Their faces were elongated eggs, smeared with age, mascara, and the torrid pain of women scorned. They were displayed in all black, from their hoary heads down to their weather-worn feet. I went cold as a tombstone. Their haggard emotions were vailed in mourning. Each carried a beautiful, colorful treasure chest, designed to safekeep their most precious memories of life. Individually, one after another, without concession, the broken ones approached me in the long corridor and aligned their bodies uniformly with their treasure chest in their hands. Their silence was piercing. I knew it was for me to open the treasure chests. And, somehow, I also knew I was the person who had given the treasure chests to the sorrowing line of antiquated widows. The line was endless as the corridor itself. One by one, I opened the boxes. They

were all the same inside – empty. Ravished by the
whirlwind: broken, barren, and beguiled.

"What is this?" I thought to myself. "What is
going on? I've got to get out of here!"

But there was no way out. No turning back.
As I moved forward, the corridor behind me
disappeared. I had to finish my pilgrimage whether
I wanted to or not. I continued trekking the long
corridor.

OH GOD, HELP ME.

"Words like doors open with ease, with very, very
little keys, and don't forget the two of these: "I
thank you," or "If you please."

Mom!

All the hoary headed matrons were crying
my name aloud.

Kevin...

Kevin...

Kavone...

Then it hit me. I knew who they were. Girls,
hotties as I referred to them. Their youthful looks

were gone. I robbed them of their youthful fortune with my smooth, satiny lies. I transformed the young, beautiful girls to old, embittered, empty, unfulfilled women.

One of the old ladies, standing afar in the distance, and disconnected from the endless line of old ladies, made her way to me. She had another small package with a bow on it and pushed it in my direction.

"No!" I said. "Get away from me old lady. I don't want it. Please leave!"

"Opin et, Kavon!"

"Her voice was cracking and worn, but still familiar. I know her accent, her tone."

"Opin et." She said again, while coughing profusely...

MOM! HELP! JESUS! HELP ME!

"Evone after ole dis time, you still note listen to me, Kavone. Hea, take et, opin et." Coughing heavily.

"Oh wow..., Bijon. Is that you?"

My heart turned white as the sparsely placed strands of hair upon her head. I shivered in remorse. I couldn't bear looking at her that way. I could tell life was relentlessly cruel to her. All the spirit she once had was gone.

"Don't be afraid, child. Look inside."

I took a deep breath and hesitantly reached for the sacred box cradled in her trembling, palsied hand. I was pushed back by horror when the contents were revealed.

"Yes, Kavone. Twins. Two sets. I miscarry two time in the midst of our turbulent relation. Just like some of the other girls who miscarry your childs, or abort dem. You miss so much, Kavone. Even when you spill your seed upon the ground, Kavone, et is note good. You hut me. I cry very hard. Cry long time. Never stop cry to dis day. I still crying. I loss everyting to you, Kavone. I loss my love in the hart. My hart is a seed not ever grow. Et die. Like our childs die. No love in der." Bijon was tapping the place on her chest where her heart once resided.

"You take et frome me, Kavone. You note give et back. My hart was love to only you. But et die all alone. Et is no comfort. I die lonely life. Same as I live." Coughing profusely.

I continued gazing at the four dead fetuses in the small gift box. They were small as a baby frog and quiet as a sheet of paper with no words to share. They were quieter than my tears. My tears were speechless. They had no words to say, no speech to give. My tears stayed in the corners of my eyes and caused my tongue to fold like a towel and retreat to the deep, meaty part of my throat. I swallowed the remaining air in my mouth. My children are dead. They did not have so much as an obituary. They had no parting words. Their welcoming into this world was cold as a frozen twig broken from a tree, buried in a small frozen pond. They did not know the love of their father. They *came and then they were gone. Oh, what withered hand the writer has.*

"Bijon, I did not know."

"I know dis, Kavone. You could note have known et. All of et was a big ole game to you. But I was note play. I true love with you. You toss me to the garbage and I rot my whole life. Now move frome my face. Go back to your life. Egare! Go frome me, Kavone."

MOM!!!!!!!!!!

That feeling of peace and tranquility has been hijacked by my wrong doings, by my sins, my bad choices, my selfishness. I jaded all those innocent girls. Ruined all those precious lives. Told all those cold, heartless lies. And made all those empty promises, and thought nothing of it. Bijon was right. It was a joke to me. It was a part of the game. It's what I did. "Man..."

My countenance fell.

There was a majestic, bright, light at the end of the corridor. All I knew was I needed to get to the light. I felt that I would be safe if I could make it to the light. But the darkness was thick, I could feel it groping my body, gripping me tighter and tighter as I tried to sprint toward the light. It was holding me back. Judging me, convicting me, sentencing me. Killing me.

I focused all my energy on the gravity of the light's compelling brilliance but my past caught up with me and whispered, "It is time to pay."

I found myself reaching out to the light, praying that it could be grabbed by my mortal hands and reeled in.

The other girls, forsaken and disconsolate, along with Bijon, cried louder and louder. My heart pounded lifelessly. I began running but could not escape their cries. Their pain was all over me. It was in every thought, every memory, and in every desire to make amends.

AAAAHHHHHHH!!!!

I MESSED UP!

This was a ghastly ghost story. My story. The girls were decaying and mummifying, running behind me whaling, seeking answers.

"Why Kevin, WHY!!!?"

I continued screaming and running toward the light. But it began to fade as I drew closer to it until it was totally out of my sight and poof! It was gone. The light was gone.

"NOOOOO! Come back! Please, come back..."

The light refused to shine. She continued hiding her white face from the blackness of my sins.

***

MY EYES POP WIDE OPEN...

A beautiful young nurse was standing before me smiling with a pillow in her hand.

"Relax, Mr. Washington. You are in recovery now. Everything was successful! Your surgery was a complete success! We are so proud of you! The doctors did everything! They pulled out all the stops! And here you are, being made whole. Wow! The Big Guy was truly looking out for you! My name is Ms. Bonita and I will be your nurse for today!"

I looked around the room trying to regain my bearings. The long corridor, the old women, Bijon! The twins. MY TWINS! MOM! MAN!!!, MY CHILDREN! They were gone! They were all gone. The bright light, the treasure chests, the gift box. All of it… gone. I scanned the room further looking for all the crazy doctors and nurses that were trying to kill me and use me as an experiment. I looked for the experimental dungeon they wanted to drag me too. But it was not there. It was gone. They were gone. All of it was gone. **I dreamed it all!**

A DREAM. WAS IT A DREAM? WAS IT REALLY ALL JUST A DREAM? NAH… IT COULDN'T BE. IT WAS REAL. IT HAD TO BE REAL. HOW COULD IT BE JUST A DREAM. I

WAS THERE. I SAW IT. I SAW THEM. ALL OF THEM. THEY WERE THERE. I SAW MY LIFE. IT FLASHED BEFORE ME. I SAW THE LIGHT, THE CORRIDOR. I SAW BIJON! I SAW MY WHOLE LIFE. AND NOW, WHERE DID IT GO? AS I LOOK AROUND, ALL I SEE IS A QUIET ROOM, NICELY LIT, WITH MEDICAL EQUIPMENT SURROUNDING ME. THEN I REALIZE IT WAS TRULY ALL JUST A DREAM.

But I knew it would be with me a lifetime. I will never forget that feeling, that deflated feeling in my heart.

I was still delirious and incoherent from the anesthesia. I tried to get out of bed so that I could go home and tell my mom of all that happened. My legs did not cooperate! I tried lifting them again, and still, they were calling the shots! And then I remembered!

AAAAHHHHHHH!!!!

MY LEGS ARE STINGING!

The doctor finally calmed me down. The nurse patted my head dry and gave me a cup of chipped ice. The doctor explained with great sympathy, that, I was indeed paralyzed, but also explained with great enthusiasm, that, the pain that I was feeling was a good sign. It meant that my nerve endings were still alive, which bore the strong possibility and likelihood of me regaining the use of my legs.

I was so grateful to hear such promising news. The accident was fresh in my mind. I remembered everything. I couldn't stop the tears from flowing. My soul wept. In a split second, I was totally clueless of my future. I was no longer The Wash, The Chill, Teddy P.

Why would I have such a heart-rattling vision? Was I really that bad? How could I have sunken so low? How could I have become so base, so bane, so barren. Suddenly, I was more barren than any woman. There was no fruit in my life worth mentioning. Having a college degree, being engaged to a beautiful vixen, being so popular, and going pro no longer mattered. Those were small things in comparison to how badly I had behaved my entire adult life. The visions revealed that my bad far outweighed my good, and it was too heavy a cross for me to bear. The pressures of life broke me. I pondered more scrutinizingly the things I saw in my night visions.

I had a spiritual awakening.

BUT IT'S NOT FAIR!

WHAT ABOUT ME?!!!

I DIDN'T DO THIS BY MYSELF!!!

My life was torn to pieces.

I made a mess of things.

My relationships were a wreck.

I used girls like I did not have a mother.

BUT IT WASN'T JUST ON ME!

THEY WANTED IT TOO!

WHY AM I THE FALL GUY?

WHY!!!

I was a known liar and cheat.

I had become a failure.

I was not supposed to be this guy!

I had loving parents...

Wholesome friends and family...

And a wonderful church family that
advocated the Scriptures and living thereby.

I blew it all.

I was going to college...

Preparing for pro ball...

About to get married...

And approaching graduation...

I had only two weeks to go before walking
across the stage with a Psychology Degree.

And with all that I had accomplished,
It was clear to me that I had not begun
living. I knew there was more.

There was more to life than I had
discovered.

All of the partying...

All of the skirt chasing...

All of the money wasted on equipment...

I was still as empty as a bank account with a zero balance.

I was at the bottom...

I needed change...

I began taking my voyage of soul searching seriously...

My life was truly a mess.

I laid in bed with my head

towards the sky and thought,

It's time to clean it up.

✳✳✳

"Well hello, Mr. Washington! It's a beautiful day today! Let me open your blinds so that you can absorb some of these wonderful sunrays! I can't let a handsome young man like you lay around feeling sorry for yourself. It's time to live! Have a fresh start! New beginnings! I am nurse Agatha, and I will be your nurse today and every day, if you request me. I am here to help you in any way I can. And Mr. Washington..."

I turned toward her direction.

"Yes, nurse?"

"I do mean anything," she said, while lightly pursing her lips and stroking her neck softly.

She made my stomach turn. I gave her a puzzled look and asked, "Where is Nurse Bonita? Is she on duty today?"

"Nurse Bonita? Nah, she off on Tuesday and Wednesday. I'm yo' nurse, okay."

I turned my head away from her and began staring back into the sky, pondering my fresh start, the one that does not include a nurse Agatha! However, these antics continued throughout the next few days. Nurse Agatha, and a few more female staff members were throwing themselves at me and I didn't quite understand why, until I noticed the stack of business cards on the nightstand next to my bed. Countless lawyers had been to my room when I was still affected by the anesthesia and not fully conscious of my environment. My case was rumored to be worth a whopping $5,000,000. This news was quickly spreading throughout the hospital, and a few of the vultures were swarming around waiting to sink their fangs into the juicy money-green steak.

As soon as hospital administration realized what was going on, they put a screeching halt to the commercialization of my case and focused on getting me well again.

Physical therapy was the easy part of my healing. But the emotional reconstruction was painstaking. The trajectory of my entire life had changed in the blink of my eyes. I had just spent the last 4 years preparing for a career that would have me set for life. I was almost there, with only two weeks to go. It came crashing down in the worst way. Life as I planned it would never be. All I knew, or wanted to know was football. Now, in a matter of seconds, I would never play again.

I DIDN'T HAVE A CHANCE.

I WAS GOING TO CHANGE.

THIS IS TOO MUCH!

I CAN'T WALK!

THIS IS NOT FAIR!!!

AAAAHHHHHHH!!!!

My stay in the hospital was a strenuous nine months long. My eyes were filled with water each and every day.

Every time I saw someone walking, or a couple holding hands, or a group of athletes rushing to see a fellow teammate that has been injured, brought tears to my eyes. I had no legs, no fiancé, and no fellow teammates rushing me with support. My heart heaved with heaviness. There was no comfort for me. Everything in each passing day was a reminder of what I lost.

LEGS

LOST

FRIENDS

LOST

POPULARITY

LOST

YOUTH

LOST

HOPE

LOST

MAN! IT'S NOT FAIR!

WHY IS THIS HAPPENING TO ME!

AAAAHHHHHHH!!!!

FAMILY

LOST

The nurses turned me regularly.

"Afternoon, Mr. Washington. I am here to turn you on your other side for a while. I hope you have been having a good day. The sun is shining bright out there. Do you want me to sit you up in a chair and push you in front of the window?"

"NOPE."

AUTONOMY

LOST

SENSE OF VALUE

LOST

OPPORTUNITY

LOST

A FEELING OF PEACE

LOST

DIRECTION

LOST

CAREER

LOST

WHY?!!!

WHY?!!!

ONE MONTH.

TWO MONTHS.

THREE MONTHS.

FOUR MONTHS.

HAVE COME AND GONE.

AND STILL,

NO ANSWERS.

WHY?!

I pushed hard and out came a solid, mahogany log and landed perfectly in the middle of my adult diaper. I pushed hard again and out squished chocolate cream. It filled the entire diaper and any gaps between my legs.

AAAAHHHHHHH!!!!

I pushed again and again and again.

AAAAHHHHHHH!!!!

Murky, swamp smelling waters skeeted straightway onto the pile of soft chocolate and callous log. A melting mess of dark brown and darker brown oozed out of my diaper. I lay there crying silently, twisting my chocolate cream stained sheets into an angry knot, hating every day that my sorrowing eyes opened to this unfair fate.

AAAAHHHHHHH!!!!

PURPOSE

LOST

MANHOOD

LOST

PRIDE

LOST

JOY

LOST

MYSELF

LOST

I was lost.

I lost myself in the game.

I thought I was on the right path.

How could I have been so far off course?

FIVE MONTHS.

SIX MONTHS.

AAAAHHHHHHHH!!!!

AAAAHHHHHHHH!!!!

AAAAHHHHHHHH!!!!

I shake the rails on the bed ferociously.

Over and over, I shake them again and again.

Brown and dark brown chocolate pong covered the bed rails.

I put my hands on the rails where the brown pong is and smear it more.

AAAAHHHHHHHH!!!!

Nurrrrrrse!

No one came to my rescue.

They were waiting for me to calm down.

Nurse!

Nurse!

AAAAHHHHHHH!!!!

Nurrrrrrse!

Somebody get in here and clean me up

NOW!

I scream at the top of my lungs.

Nurrrrrrse!

The nurses are tired of my shenanigans.

They have had enough.

Seven months was enough for them.

I snatch all the blankets and pillows off my

bed and toss them to the floor.

They were covered in pong.

AAAAHHHHHHH!!!!

I CAN'T WALK.

I CAN'T PLAY BALL.

I CAN'T DO NOTHING!!!

I CAN'T LIVE LIKE THIS!!!

I CAN'T BREATHE.

I'm out of breath.

I want to die.

Somebody kill me.

Please, please...

Take this life.

It isn't my life.

I don't want it!

I can't take this no more.

I'M TIRED.

I'M TIRED.

OH GOD,

I'M TIRED.

OKAY, OKAY.

I QUIT!

I GIVE UP!

I WAS WRONG!

I'M SORRRRRRYYYYY!

AAAAHHHHHHH!!!!

AAAAHHHHHHH!!!!

FORGIVE ME!

AAAAHHHHHHH!!!!

AAAAHHHHHHH!!!!

FORGIVE ME LORD.

HOW DO I MAKE THIS RIGHT?

SHOW ME WHAT TO DO?

HELP ME!

TALK TO ME!

Nurrrrrrse!

Nurrrrrrse!

✳✳✳

I was led astray by my own selfish ways.
And it felt good. But now I feel bad. All my
confidence was in a pair of worn cleats, the
number 23, plastic shoulder pads an egg-shaped
piece of pig skin that I threw really hard across an
open field. How could I have strayed so far from my
destiny? So far from life? Truly, there had to be
more for me than running up and down, back and
forth trying to avoid being knocked down or
knocking down. Lord, I cannot find my way home.

I am shaken.

How will I make a living?

How will I provide for myself?

I am afraid to make a move now.

Afraid to make a decision.

Afraid to set a goal.

Come up with a plan.

Foresee a future.

BREATHE…

I'm afraid to breathe.

I feel incompetent.

Foolish.

Like a fool.

Unsure.

Ambushed.

Discombobulated.

Stricken with grief.

BETRAYED.

I feel betrayed.

I AM LOST…

The road ahead of me is winding.

And healing is nowhere in sight.

I missed the mark by 100 miles. Nothing
that I did seemed to be the right decision.

Everything has fallen apart.

My girl is gone.

My legs are gone.

My pride is gone.

My will to live is fleeting fast.

I AM ONLY 22 YEARS OF AGE.

HOW CAN I BE PARALYZED?

I WANNA RUN!

I WANNA GO OUTSIDE!

I WANNA WALK!

AAAAHHHHHHH!!!!

AAAAHHHHHHH!!!!

WHY GOD!!!

GOD WHY!!!

GOD!!!

WHY WON'T YOU TALK TO ME!!!

My eyes were swollen as grandma's ankles.
I could not see the rest of days. My future was
bleak and dismal. The Seattle Hawks forgot about
me the day they learned I lay upon a gurney. I
never received another call.

I WAS LEFT FOR DEAD.

SO, TELL ME, IF YOU HAVE AN INKLING,

WHAT IS LIFE?

***

"Good news, Mr. Washington," the doctor said. "You have been making excellent progress with your physical therapy. And your updated X-rays show substantial healing in your back. It's looking good for you. We have another specialist coming in who is going to restructure your physical therapy to concentrate on some of the weaker areas in the X-ray results. If you follow the plan, and do just what the doctor prescribes, we can have you out of here and going home in the next sixty days!

Chapter 13

The Prayer, The Praise, The Exhortation

Let the word of Christ dwell in you richly in all wisdom;
teaching and admonishing one another in psalms and
hymns and spiritual songs, singing with grace in your hearts
to the Lord.

Colossians 3:16

LAST NIGHT OF SUMMER REVIVAL

"Saints, let's give a warm and hearty
welcome to my longtime friend, brother, and
coworker in the Lord, Pastor Kevin Washington, as
he preaches, teaches, prays, testifies, and just
comes in his own way tonight. Pastor Washington,
thank you for traveling all this way to close out our
summer revival. You bless us every year. Your

continued support and faithfulness is a great honor and shall never be for gotten. Church, stand to your feet and help me welcome my friend as he comes."

CONGREGATIONAL OVATION AND HEARTFELT APPLAUSE...

"Thank you, Pastor. My wife and I are always excited about being invited to fellowship with you. We don't feel like guests. You and your entire congregation always make us feel right at home."

SEVERAL MEMBERS SHOUT "AMEN!" SEVERAL HAND CLAPS WISK THROUGH THE ROOM.

"But, before we go any further brothers and sisters, shall we bow our heads and pray?"

AMEN, BROTHER...

"Father in the name of Jesus. A name which is above every name. We come before you giving thanks for what you have done, what you are doing, and what you are going to do. There is none like you. We ask that you word the mouth of this, thine vessel, tonight. Anoint from the crown of my head, even down to the very soles of my feet. Let your people be blessed. You see every need in the room. You see what we cannot see. You feel what we cannot feel. Feel the infirmities of your people tonight. Speak to hearts. Let someone hear something that will make them say within their hearts, "What must I do to be saved?" We pray that someone will be touched in the way that only you can touch. Speak healing to lost souls tonight. Mend broken hearts, broken homes, broken marriages, and broken lives. Someone has had it up to here. They have been facing setback after setback, disappointment after disappointment. They are tired. They feel like the pressure of life is going to crush them. FATHER! Look on your people tonight. Send comfort. Send rest. Speak peace. Deliver those that are bound by spirits of darkness like only you can deliver. Those that are in the midst of turmoil, calm the raging sea in their lives. You see every toxic relationship. Every battered woman, every abused child. You are omniscient, omnipresent. You are a very present help in the time of trouble. You can fix that situation. Those who are tied to someone who does not want or appreciate your Word or the lifestyle that you have called us to live... those who are unequally yoked... You can fix it, Lord. We depend on you. Lord through your Word tonight. Convict those who have said with their mouths that they are yours, but their hearts are far from you. Father, touch those that are looking for love and life in all the wrong places. Shift the trajectory of someone's life tonight. So, as we go forth tonight in your Word, convict, convince, and convert. In The Mighty Name of Jesus we pray. Thank God. Thank God! And Aaaaamen."

EVERYONE IN THE BUILDING IS PRAISING AND WORSHIPPING GOD!

"Amen, amen. God Bless You Now! As I said, earlier, I am always grateful to be a part of your services and to have the opportunity to fellowship with you whether it is in a special service, or, simply enjoying a short weekend vacation. Spending time with you is just like being at home. And as a testimony of your hospitality that even beats being at home, my wife and I were just discussing last night before we went to bed how good the food is! Man! My God! This down-home cooking is spoiling us! It's like some people say, the food is so good it will make you slap your Momma!

LOUD LAUGHTER FILLS THE ROOM!

Praise God that my mother is already in Glory, because I sure would not want to be sent to an early grave for slapping my mother over this delicious mouthwatering southern fried chicken, creamy macaroni and cheese, homemade cornbread with the big, plump sweet corn in it, potato salad made with those premium baby potatoes, handpicked turnips and mustards with the pot liquor sitting over there on the counter next to the window calling my name, pot roast, fresh fried okra, fried freshwater catfish, shrimp, black-eyed peas, green beans, and any kind of dessert I can think of. My God, my God! Ooooweee.

SAINTS ARE LAUGHING, OOING AND AAHING...

Truly, we are grateful for your generous hospitality and kindness, saints. Truly, we can't ask for more.

But moving on... Some of you may know, and some of you may not know, your Pastor and I have a long history together. Our paths intersected way back in my college days, some 25 – 30 years ago. He is a couple years older than I am so he had already graduated from college. But he was a young activist back then. He was saved and living for God and had a desire to give back to his community. I was at one of his rallies and he touched my life way back then. We talked for only a moment but I was indelibly influenced by his passion for people and helping others. I knew he thought I wasn't going to make it because I was so caught up in the world trying to grasp fame and fortune. I was only thinking about helping myself. No one else, just me. But look at God! I am here, a living witness and testimony of the Love, Mercy, Longsuffering, and Miracle Working Power of God, through The Saving Grace of His Wonderful, Adored Son, Christ Jesus, My Lord and Personal Savior.

Now, my passion is to help the community and share The Word of God, just like your fine pastor. God knew that we would meet again. His labor was not in vain. The Scripture says that one watereth, another planteth, but God gives the increase. I am so glad that our paths intersected all those years ago. Who knew that we would end up as coworkers in the ministry together? Isn't God good!"

THE CONGREGATION SHOUTS AMEN!

"God has called me and I am submitted and willing to share The Word of God with you. May we all be edified! Amen!"

AMEN…

"Hasn't this been a wonderful week of revival?"

AMEN, PASTOR!

"If you have enjoyed yourself this week and you have gotten your breakthrough, give God some praise."

RIOTOUS PRAISES FILL THE ROOM!

"Yes, yes! I like what I am hearing. That's right, fill this room with praise! You see, that's why I like coming here. I don't have to work up a praise in you. You have a praise down on the inside. You came to praise God! This is a church where you know how to praise the Lord! Y'all the kind of folks I like to worship with. Go ahead, Lift Him up! Praises are comely with the saints!"

MORE RIOTOUS PRAISES FILL THE ROOM!

"One day I heard somebody say, when I think of the goodness of Jesus, and all he has done for me, my soul cries out, Hallelujah! Praise God for saving me!

SOME SAINTS ARE SHOUTING AND
DANCING AGAIN! THE PRAISES ARE HIGH!

"Oooh, God bless you now! Look what I
have started. You all are about to start something
up in here. But that's all right. Jesus started this
thing over 2,000 years ago! This ain't nothing new.
Come on organist, give me some shouting music.
Praise Him with a dance, saints! Praise Him on the
high-sounding symbols. Praise Him on the drums,
Praise Him with the tambourine, Praise Him with
the trumpet. Praise Him. Praise Him. Let everything
that hath breath, praise ye The Lord!!!"

More congregants stand, while others leap
to their feet praising and worshiping God. They fill
the isles and gather in the pews. Men, women and
children are dancing to the joyous sound, Jesus
Saves! THERE IS SHOUTING ROOM ONLY!

"That's right people, praise Him for what he
has done! He brought you from a mighty long way.

Remember, David praised Him with all of his might. Come on, let's give it all we've got tonight.

Somebody needs a healing in their body. It's in the praise. Somebody has lost their way and needs their faith restored. It's in the praise. Somebody has lost focus and does not know their purpose in life. Somebody needs a financial blessing. It's in the praise. Somebody needs the Holy Ghost. He's in the praise. If you need more power. Power is in the praise! Make a joyful noise unto The Lord! The joy of The Lord is your strength! You have a right to praise The Lord!

All of us were lost in trespasses and sin and needed a Savior. There is no God like unto our God! Holy and Righteous is HIS Name. His name alone is a strong tower. The righteous can run into it and be safe! Call on Him. That's right. Call on His Name. JESUS! If you haven't gotten your break through, you better get it now!

Y'all better stop! Wait a minute, wait a minute. It's too late. HE'S ALREADY HERE. HE'S IN THE ROOM. GIVE HIM THE GLORY!

LIFT UP HIS NAME!

JESUS, JESUS, JESUS!

GIVE HIM THE HIGHEST PRAISE!

HALLELUJAH!

GLORY HALLELUJAH!

HE'S WORTHY!

WORTHY OF THE HONOR!

WORTHY OF THE PRAISE!

HALLELUJAH!

Okay, okay.

Laughing...

Y'all better stop and let me preach in here tonight. You see, there was a time in life I was lost. I mean totally lost. I want you to hear me tonight. It's a terrible thing to be lost and not know that you are lost. Do you realize how far out of the way you can go when you are lost and not know you are lost? Do you know how far you can veer from the path that God has planned for you when you do not realize you have left the path?

Listen to me, saints of God. I grew up in a home where salvation and righteous living was preached and taught. My mother was saved. My father was saved. My uncle was saved. I went to church every day of the week. Thank God for wisdom these days. Now that I am a pastor, I do not keep my people in church every day of the week. Come on now."

AMEN... SAINTS LAUGHING LIGHTHEARTEDLY.

No wonder the young people hated church back in my day. Church was punishment to us! We would ask the simplest questions and church was always the answer!

Mom, can I go outside and play with my friends?"

NOOO, you cannot go outside and play with your friends, I'm about to take you to church.

Mom, can I watch T.V.?

NOOO, boy, turn that T.V. off. Go put your church clothes on. We are about to leave.

Mom! There's a neighborhood picnic in the park. Can I go? They are giving away free hotdogs.

NOOO, we have food. I already cooked. I don't want you to mess up your appetite. Now let's go. It's time for church!

CONGREGANTS CONTINUE LAUGHING AT THE LIGHTHEARTED COMEDIC RELIEF...

But seriously saints, it's a terrible thing to not know that you are lost. Or even worse, to feel like you are being forced to do something that you don't really want to do. You may have your eyes all set on going left. But you are told to go right. Come on somebody.

Even as a child, I felt like my life was my life. And I wanted to do what I wanted to do with it. I didn't want to be going to no church every single day. Come on now, somebody. Where are my young people? Young folks, can I get an amen?

YOUNG ADULTS AND ADULTS LAUGH AND SAY AMEN.

"Listen, let me ask you a question. Have you ever been caught up in doing something and wanted to stop but could not stop? Have you ever been so disturbed by your actions and the things that you were doing but still kept doing them?

There was a time in life where I lost my absolute mind. I was running around fornicating myself to death. It took God allowing me to get in a near fatal accident which left me paralyzed from the waist down. I promise you I was not fornicating then. I couldn't, even if I wanted to; and I did want to.

Don't let God stop you.

I want you to hear me in this house tonight.

I had every opportunity to amend my ways.
I was warned but I wouldn't listen. I was
sneaking out of church at 10 years old. I was
being deceitful, disobedient, conniving, and
hardheaded. Thinking I was outsmarting
and out slicking my parents and God.
I was doing my own thing. But the only
person I outsmarted and outslicked was
myself.
DISOBEDIENCE IS A SETUP...
LISTEN TO ME...
Children, obey your parents...
Young people, stay in school...
Husbands and wives, be temperate in all
things...
Don't go outside of your marriage...
DON'T DO IT...
IT'S A SETUP!
I was being setup to be unruly, defiant,
stubborn, and willful. I was being setup to be lost.

I cheated myself out of a strong, productive youth. I was cut down at the age of 22. The age when young people are just beginning to truly live. I was fighting for my next breath, trying to hold on to any glimmer of life, and what was left of it.

But somehow, in the midst of it all, I knew God was changing the trajectory of my life. With my back and legs being hijacked into paralysis, I became angry, bitter and sad. The things I enjoyed so much were now a thing of the past. I would not have chosen a wheelchair. But I had no say in the matter. However, once I began to respond differently to my brazen circumstances, through faith they became strengths that propelled me to the next level in life. I began to enjoy my new path, living righteously and soberly. I felt good about helping others, leading young people down the right path, sharing how my story of self-will put my life in an unnecessary chokehold. Soon, overwhelming feelings of loss and regret, depression, anger, guilt and pain, were replaced with hope, purpose, happiness, peace, forgiveness, and contentment.

It's been thirty plus years since that life-changing, near fatal crash on that rainy evening of, Friday, March 26, 1983. Let the people of The Lord say, Praise the Lord!"

PRAISE THE LORD!!!

"Yes! Unexpected Tragedy... Painful Affliction... Insurmountable Brokenness, can all be blessings in disguise... Yes! Unexpected Tragedy can become the catalyst to Triumph in Hope and Faith. Painful Affliction can become a Victorious Testimony of Strength and Courage. And, Insurmountable Brokenness, a broken back, along with paralysis, can become a lifelong, life-changing experience of Healing, Resilience and Restoration. All of these experiences lead me to one pressing question...

Chapter 14

What Is Life?

Remember now thy Creator in the days of thy youth, while
the evil days come not, nor the years draw nigh, when thou
shalt say, I have no pleasure in them; Let us hear the
conclusion of the whole matter: Fear God, and keep his
commandments: for this is the whole duty of man. For God
shall bring every work into judgment, with every secret
thing, whether it be good, or whether it be evil.

Ecclesiastes 12: 1, 13-14

THE MESSAGE OF THE HOUR

Now that God has restored my mind, I have

transitioned from all the distractions and the

foolishness that Satan had planted in my heart. I no

longer call myself The Chill Factor, Teddy P., The

Wash, or any other crazy name assigned to me. I now live by faith and not by the false security found in popularity. I use the name that my mother gave me and the title that God has assigned. Saints, Elder Kevin Washington stands before you today, humbly by faith. It is no goodness of my own. God saved me. And there is not much left that can be said or done. I once was living a life that He did not design for me. It took God stopping me in my tracks so that I could become aware of my grave folly and repent, and begin anew, and live the prosperous, peaceful life that He purposed in the very beginning of His thoughts of me. So, let's get into the message and delve into that one pressing question.

What Is Life?

When this question is posed on intellectual platforms and otherwise, often the immediate response is to render a definition. However, this message is not about the definition of the word life, but rather, the source and purpose of life.

Tonight, I pray God gives us a revelation regarding the answer to this perplexing question. This question has manufactured marvel in the minds of mankind for innumerable millennia. Many theologians, scientists, and authorities have attempted to answer this question to their own dismay. At best, some have given accurate definitions, but somehow those definitions ring out as inadequate and do not disclose the core, purpose, or true meaning of life. It has been stated that some fledgling philosophers fold in their quest to bottle the essence of life by only producing a scientific explanation, nothing more. Biologists have superficially defined it as the condition that distinguishes plants and animals from inorganic matter. Medical researchers have defined it as the capacity for growth, reproduction and eventual death. Humanists define life as the condition of indulging in the arts, in socio-emotional communities, and in all things conducive to human growth and development. Philosophers and psychologists define life as the ability to think and be aware of oneself. *I think, therefore I am - Rene Decartes.* In their conclusions, they declare that life is anything that comes into existence, grows and dies. They say life is activity... energy... movement... vitality... vigor... and vivacity. When life is present, it is said that mental wheels are turning, ideas are brimming, thoughts are flowing fluidly. They say you have enthusiasm and are filled with excitement. These are all signs that the professionals identify to say that you have life.

Also, these passionate professionals, in their schools of thought, push past scientific definitions and become deeply intimate with their research. These relentless scholars say life is the soul of man; the intelligent, immaterial, immortal part of human beings. They say that life is spirit... the nonphysical part of a person which is the seat of emotions and character. It is regarded as the true self, the part of man's self that survives physical death and bodily separation.

232

The definitions go on and on, from person to person, discipline to discipline. But they all have one thing in common: THEY ARE WRONG. Or, maybe I should say, they all fall short of the whole truth.

Life, in its truest essence, cannot be wholly defined by any amount of human knowledge or discourse. Tonight, what I have done to give more knowledge about the meaning of life, is to first expound upon what life is not according to The Scriptures, which is The Word of Life. Hopefully, this knowledge will lead us closer to comprehending what life is.

So again, I internalize and process the concept of What Is Life by first acknowledging and accepting what life is not.

I acknowledge and accept that life is not mine. 1st Corinthians 6: 19-20, states, "What? know ye not that your body is the temple of the Holy Ghost which is in you, which ye have of God, and ye are not your own? For ye are bought with a price: therefore, glorify God in your body, and in your spirit, which are God's."

Many people struggle with that stark truth. Youth, in all their folly, will foolishly look their parents in their eyes, and proclaim with their loudest, most convicting voice of all, "This is my life. Why are you trying to run me!" And in kind, the same is true for adults. When feeling overwhelmed by demands and instructions, many adults find themselves exasperated with these overwhelming thoughts, "I am grown! I'm an adult! I pay my own bills! No one controls me! I make my own decisions! Leave me alone. THIS IS MY LIFE!!! You're not the boss of me!"

Yes! We all struggle one way or another when submitting our will to the will of authorities who govern over us. How much more to the will of God that is the total opposite of our will? The scripture states in Galatians 5:17, "For the flesh lusteth against the Spirit, and the Spirit against the flesh: and these are contrary the one to the other: so that ye cannot do the things that ye would."

Even the Apostle Paul, after being smitten with blindness for three days on the road to Damascus and seeing a great light, and giving his life to God, no longer requesting letters giving him the right to waste the church of God, even after giving his life wholly to God, forsaking all, to follow Christ, found himself saying, "O wretched man that I am! who shall deliver me from the body of this death?" Somewhere upon his journey of transformation, while in that great city of Corinth, he wrote a letter to the saints in Rome, which we call the Book of Romans. It is the longest letter that Paul wrote. A small passage reads as follows:

14 For we know that the law is spiritual: but I am carnal, sold under sin.

15 For that which I do I allow not: for what I would, that do I not; but what I hate, that do I.

16 If then I do that which I would not, I consent unto the law that it is good.

17 Now then it is no more I that do it, but sin that dwelleth in me.

18 For I know that in me (that is, in my flesh,) dwelleth no good thing: for to will is present with me; but how to perform that which is good I find not.

19 For the good that I would I do not: but the evil which I would not, that I do.

20 Now if I do that I would not, it is no more I that do it, but sin that dwelleth in me.

21 I find then a law, that, when I would do good, evil is present with me.

22 For I delight in the law of God after the inward man:

23 But I see another law in my members, warring against the law of my mind, and bringing me into captivity to the law of sin which is in my members.

24 O wretched man that I am! who shall deliver me from the body of this death?

Romans 7:14-24

There is a war going on down on the inside of Paul's heart. Paul discovers the law of the two natures. He learns that he will love one and hate the other... obey one and transgress against the other. Paul understands that one of the natures is the Godly nature. He also knows that the Godly nature is good for him and is exactly what he needs. However, Paul finds himself still yearning for that other nature. That fleshy, unruly, unorthodox, unrefined, unsavory, ungodly nature... Paul is not deceived in the least bit. He understands that the old nature is still within his members but must be denied. Paul realizes that his old nature is depraved and is only GOOD TO HIS OLD MAN and not good FOR his renewed, self-submitted life to God. Paul was declaring that his life was not his own. He knew that he could not do what he wants to do, when he wants to do it, like he wants to do it. He acknowledges, "This is not life!" He, in fact, declares, "O wretched man that I am. Who shall deliver me from this body of death…"

Well, today we know who The Deliverer is. Sometimes we have to cry out, "Deliver me!"

Right where you are sitting, cry out from the depths of your soul, "Deliver me!" Some in the building tonight are still taunted and held captive by the sins of their past. Say, "Deliver me, God!"

Don't be ashamed, tonight.

Cry out, Deliver me! Deliver me, God!"

Let God know that you are tired.

Tired of being shackled.

Shackled by lust.

Lust of the flesh.

Flesh of strange women.

Women that are lewd.

Lewd, indulgent women.

Women that have the power to take you to that place of no return.

Return to the ark of safety, tonight.

Tonight, cry out if you feel you are reaching
that place of no return...
 You can't leave your wife, man.
Do you know what that will do to your
family?
To your children?
To your daughters?
Your sons?
It is time to cry out to God.
Right where you are sitting, all across this
building, cry out to God, and say...
"Deliver me, Oh God. Deliver me!"
The truth of the matter is He will deliver
you because we all belong to God and it is not His
will that any of us should perish. We hijack our lives
when we make the decision to live in a manner
that is contrary to the will of God.

To truly answer the question, "What Is
Life?", we must accept the fact that our life belongs
to God. He created us to do of His will and good
pleasure.

Tonight, you are looking at a man who once lived life recklessly, to do of his own degenerate pleasures. I was not thinking about God. I was thinking about the ladies, and how I could make them all mine. I was thinking about football and how football would make me a lady magnet. I was thinking how a prestigious career would make me popular, famous and rich. God was not in the picture – at all. That was not life. As a matter of fact, that almost killed me.

I did not create myself. I did not give myself life. I did not will myself into being. Therefore, I do not own the rights to do as I please with my life. Life is not mine. There is a grave difference between what belongs to me and what belongs to God. Can we say amen?

AMEN…

I also had to learn, that, according to Luke 12:23, "Life is more than meat, and the body is more than raiment."

In other words, life is not just about me meeting my fleshly needs and desires. The Scripture says that it is in Him we live, move and have our being. Sure, food, clothing, and shelter are necessities and we must have those things to mitigate our way through life comfortably. And yes, bodily exercise is a requirement if one is to be healthy. However, even Maslow's hierarchy of needs stretches beyond the personal foundational requirements of life. Maslow's theory speaks of self-actualization, the concept of moving beyond one's personal needs and becoming an individual that focuses upon helping others. Life should not be consumed with acquiring personal comforts... personal needs. That's what Esau did and lost everything. Because of his selfishness he ended up with nothing. Esau sold his birthright to satisfy a selfish thought. My God, how many times did we make the wrong decision just because of a selfish thought...

I thought I needed that expensive new car...

That fine woman...

A stiff drink...

That next high...

I thought I needed just one more hit...

Success was a drug.

I thought I needed that promotion more

than anything else in the world...

I thought I needed to enter a new tax

bracket by any means necessary...

Some of us thought we needed revenge...

We thought we needed to hold grudges...

Tell lies...

Gossip...

Backbite...

Snitch...

Become talebearers...

We thought we needed an edge...

An angle...

We thought if we could only be accepted...

We thought if we could only fit in...

Be popular...

Be the head of this auxiliary, that auxiliary...

Sing in the choir...

Lead this song, that song...

Marry this brother, that sister...

All these foolish thoughts were bombarding our minds...

Say amen in this house tonight.

Aaaah yes. God is here...

And He's speaking to us.

It's time to stop fussing and fighting in the church... Treating God's church like it's a Gladiator tournament.

Why are we vying for positions?

You know, as people of ambition, we can go off in those ambitions. A thing can get personal to us, even selfish. It can become about us.

When did God's Church become Man's Church...? When did it become a political institution? A place for pushing personal interests? We may need to examine the Pecking Order...

Why are we competing for positions the way the world competes?

Why are we trying to keep the highest ranks in our personal family?

Voting and politicking for our friends...

Seeking recognition...

Trying to make a name for ourselves...

Did God not warn us regarding seeking and giving flattering titles unto men?

What makes us think God will approve of us doing the opposite of His will? Do we honestly think He is pleased with our actions... our motives... our behavior? Do we really believe that God is looking down on us in pleasure when we walk and live contrary to His Word and will?

WHAT IS LIFE?

WHAT ARE YOU DOING WITH YOUR LIFE?

Did we forget that, in His Word, God warned us about having respect of persons? Did we forget about that?

When did we get the notion that God will put his stamp of approval on that kind of behavior? It's fleshly carnality and has no place in The Church of God.

Did we forget that God warned us that there should be no schism in the body? Did we forget that He said "Let brotherly love continue?" Did we forget He said love one another?

We must not forget, saints.

We must hold on to the precepts of God's Written Holy Word.

Did you know that it is possible to be so caught up with doing our own thing that we can push God right out the door?

Man has been known to take matters into his own hands, irrespective of God's will.

Did we forget that God is the Head of The Church…?

WHAT IS LIFE?

We must go back to the Old Landmark.

It's time to do a reassessment.

We need a gut check, saints.

AMEN, PASTOR. IT'S THE TRUTH.

God is making it plain tonight.

He tells us in His Word in Psalm 75:6-7, "For promotion cometh neither from the east, nor from the west, nor from the south. But God is the judge: he putteth down one, and setteth up another." The Word tells us that God resisteth the proud and gives grace unto the humble. It's time we humble ourselves. If we really want to know what life is, we must turn to The Word of The Living God.

God never intended man's life to be squandered or consumed with foolish thoughts. He has a divine purpose for our lives. And yes, this message may feel very direct, but God loves us so much that He is taking the time to speak to us through this message. His Word states that whom the Lord loveth he chasteneth.

Our brother Job was a wealthy, God fearing man, but with a turn of events in the course of a few hours, Brother Job found himself in a world of uncertainty and asking, "What Is Life?" When all was said and done, Job concluded... "Thou has granted me life... The Spirit of God hath made me, and the breath of the Almighty hath given me life... Even our brother David, having been in the face of death innumerable times, allowed these words to pour from his lips, "For with thee *is* the fountain of life..."

"LIFE" can be summed up in one word: GOD. GOD is Life. HE is the Source of all life. Without HIM, there is nothing. End of story.

John 1:1-4a says, "In the beginning was the Word, and the Word was with God, and the Word was God. All things were made by him; and without him was not anything made that was made. In him was life..." Psalm 90: 2 states,

"Before the mountains were brought forth, or ever thou hadst formed the earth and the world, even from everlasting to everlasting, thou art God."

And finally, Acts 17:28 a,b, states, "For in him we live, and move, and have our being…"

So, what else is there? Why look any further. You have found whom your soul loves. He is here. He is in the room tonight. He is here to save your soul, to deliver you from sin. You can make this your last stop. You sought Him in the alcohol bottle, and He was not there. You sought Him in the streets, and He was not there. You have sought Him in many wicked devices, and still, He was nowhere to be found. But you can have Him tonight. And He can have you. Tonight, you can have life and have it more abundantly. You can walk in newness of life. Man has boggled his brain for eons, trying to answer that one perplexing question.

But, tonight, I challenge you. I challenge you to shift your focus from What Is Life, to *What Must I Do WITH My Life?*

What is the meaning of man's life? What are we supposed to do with our days on Earth? What assignments must we complete before we draw our last breath? What is important? What brings fulfillment? Why am I here? Why do I have life? And ultimately, "What Is Life..." All questions of this magnitude have one place to answer them completely and accurately, the Word of God. God's Word, from Genesis to Revelation, tells us the meaning of our lives, and I encourage everyone to search the Scriptures daily to see if these things are so. Our Scripture of focus for this urgent, life changing message is Ecclesiastes 12:1-2; 13-14.

> *¹Remember now thy Creator in the days of thy youth, while the evil days come not, nor the years draw nigh, when thou shalt say, I have no pleasure in them; ² While the sun, or the light, or the moon, or the stars, be*

not darkened, nor the clouds return after the rain:... [13] *Let us hear the conclusion of the whole matter: Fear God, and keep his commandments: for this is the whole duty of man.* [14] *For God shall bring every work into judgment, with every secret thing, whether it be good, or whether it be evil."*

The Word teaches us that man's whole duty is to Fear God, and keep his commandments." The simplicity of this complex instruction offers a paradox of scale and scope. While serving God is simple, the process we must undergo to do so is complex. The first verse of Ecclesiastes Chapter 12 urges us to remember our Creator while we are young. This shows that from the very start of human life our duty is to be in touch with The Spirit of God. No one is ever too young to become a servant of God. In fact, the best time to do so is in one's youth, before old age and worldly pessimism infiltrates the mind and heart (2 Timothy 3:15). Verse 2 of the Scripture refers to old age without

God in your life. Life without God is cold and dark. Life without God is life without meaning. Life without meaning is not life at all.

The 13th verse of Ecclesiastes Chapter 12 tells us to fear God and keep His commandments. To fear, in this context, means to have respect and reverence for God (Psalm 111:10, Proverbs 1:7, 9:10). It goes on to teach us how to respect and reverence God, which is done by keeping His commandments (John 1:15). We learn God's commandments by studying and living by The Word of God (Joshua 1:8, Psalm 119:11). Sometimes God speaks to us directly, and we get that "feeling" that we should or should not do something. That's a commandment from God (Matthew 4:4, 1 Kings 19:11-13). Sometimes He speaks to us through His Holy Scriptures, so it is imperative that we invest time and energy in studying God's Word. Those are commandments from God (1 Timothy 3:16). Sometimes He speaks to us through people, so we must surround ourselves with fellow servants of God. They deliver commandments from God. All of this amounts to fearing God (Isaiah 58:1, Exodus 19:3-7). Obeying what He tells us amounts to keeping His commandments. This is man's whole duty. This is man's purpose. This is the meaning of life.

In definite finality, Ecclesiastes Chapter 12 Verse 14 tells us that God is going to examine our lives and judge every action each man has committed. God Himself, a God of truth, accuracy and precision, will use His Just Scale and measure whether or not each human being has lived the meaning of life. God will weigh the good deeds and the evil and determine the eternal fate of each human soul (Psalm 9:7-8, 96:13). This Scripture admonishes us of the impending judgement for all mankind. It teaches us the importance of fulfilling the meaning of life. We must "Fear God and keep His commandments" because we will be judged by those actions. The duty of man, the meaning of life, the only thing worth living for, is to fear God and keep His commandments. Never forget to fear God and keep His commandments. That is the absolute, irrefutable meaning of life. Let it be said, let it be so.

Because of the lateness of the hour, we will not give a formal altar call. But you can repent where you sit or stand tonight. You can ask God to forgive you of your sins silently right now. If there is anyone in the house that has a mind to be saved and wants to live for God, raise your hand. If you know that at one point you were living right but have strayed away from God, and you want to be back in right fellowship with God, raise your hand. Or, if you just want to make your calling and election sure, raise your hand also.
HANDS RAISE ALL ACROSS THE ROOM. ADULTS AND YOUNG PEOPLE, ALIKE.
Shall we bow our heads and pray...

***

We praise God for The Word that He has given us tonight. We thank Him for the souls that were saved. We thank Him for those who have repented and rededicated their lives. And most of all, we thank Him for His Word. May He add a blessing to our obedience thereof. Let the church say amen.

AMEN.

Chapter 15

Thelma

"And these words, which I command thee this day, shall be in thine heart: And thou shalt teach them diligently unto thy children, and shalt talk of them when thou sittest in thine house, and when thou walkest by the way, and when thou liest down, and when thou risest up."

Deuteronomy 6:6-7

My Wife: Mrs. Thelma Tanner-Washington

THE GIRL OF MY DREAMS

1st Lady of Unity Fellowship Church of God in Christ
Licensed Cosmetologist
Designer of Custom-Made Hats
Associates of Arts Degree – Business Studies

How We Met

I met my wife November 9, 1987 in Memphis, Tennessee, during the 80th Holy Convocation of our National Church. She stood out in the midst of a crowd of young people from afar. I was drawn to her. I wanted to meet her to seek understanding as to why my attention was pulled in her direction. We had just gotten out of the first of several-to-come mid-night musicals. When I spied across the room, the melodies began playing in my head all over again.

I was with one of the young ministers heading back to our rooms when I spotted her in the crowd. All the young people were mixing and mingling. She was standing with several girls, laughing with her mouth open as wide as it could possibly open. I chuckled to myself.

I nudged the young minister with my elbow and sort of nodded with my head in the direction I wanted him to look.

"Man! Those are some beautiful sisters, brother," the young minister said while smiling and straightening his tie.

"Yes sir, they are," I replied.

"So, what are you going to do? Should we approach them?"

I stood there for a minute trying to get my lines together in my head. After stalling long enough, he bumped me with his elbow and gave me the eyebrows, lowered head, and palms up, as if to say, "What are you going to do. You ready?"

I look at him, gave him another slow nod and said, "Yes, I'm ready. Let's do this."

Immediately, fear gripped me. I could feel a bead of sweat boiling around my necktie. I stuck my finger in the top of my shirt right behind the knot of my tie. I made a minor adjustment and tried to proceed with confidence. The bead of sweat continued to multiply.

I have never been afraid of girls. Why is this so awkward?

We continue to stealthily make our way to the beautiful young women of God in our view.

Jesus, am I getting dizzy? Lord, I think I am about to pass out.

"Wait a minute, man."

"Kevin, what's up, bro?"

"Breath test…"

Chuckles… "Man, come on. You nervous? What happened to all that "Special K" stuff you told me about from back in the day?"

"I'm serious man. Breath test."

"You cool."

"No man, take a wiff!"

"Dude! You're okay," he said while leaning backwards. "I'm not about to smell your breath. If you had your gorilla on, man, I would have let you know long before this. Chill out, man, Mr. Chill Factor. Jesus!"

"Okay, okay. You are right."

My goal was to be real slick and smooth, bring my best brother rap; sound real saved, but speak to them all, so I wouldn't give myself away too early in the pursuit.

The closer we got to them, my words seemed to jumble up in my head. My one-liners became paragraphs and chapters.

KEVIN! R E L A X . . .

My mind was going faster than a spinning top. The speech that I prepared for the young lady that caught my eye had gone a mile up the road and I could not catch up...

Calm down, Kevin. You can do this. Just introduce yourself. Yeah, yeah, yeah. I'll introduce myself.

Hi, I'm Kevin Washington. They used to call me Special K... smiling while doing the bobble head.

Wham!

That's stupid. She is going to think you are stupid. Say this...

Well, hello there, young lady. It sure is a beautiful night, tonight. Want to go for a walk?

Wham!

Shut up, Kevin. It's almost one-o'clock in the morning. NO, she does not want to go outside for a walk with you. You better not ask that girl no dumb question like that.

Wham!

Mocking myself for sounding like a jerk,

It's going on one-o'clock in the morning.

WE ARE GETTING CLOSER TO THEM...

Now, I am wearing two ties. The printed one I picked for my suit and the belt of beaded sweat that has encircled my entire neck and now traveling down my chest.

Try this...

Say girl, look. I'm not for no games. I put all
that foolishness behind me when I got
saved. Do you want to be my woman? Yes
or No...
Wham!
Grrrr. Aaaahhh. THAT'S DUMB!
Nothing's working.
LORD. WHAT DO I DO!

We finally make it to the other side of the huge auditorium and are standing right in front of the three beautiful young ladies.

NOT A WORD ROLLS OFF MY TONGUE.

So much for Mr. Smooth, Debonair, Special K, The Chill Factor, Joe Wash, I Got This, Let The Master Teddy P Do His Thang!

I was mute.

Wordless.

Nonspeaking.

Tongue less.

Dumb.

Dumbfounded.

Hush up, fool.

Shut yo' mouth.

Quiet.

I was quiet as an empty football stadium,

Standing there oscillating back and forth,

brimming with a bucket full of country

cheer covering my overjoyed face.

The young minister, who accompanied me,

Minister James S. Gamble, (now Pastor) steps up to

bat and saves me. Correction…, saves the moment.

"So, tell us ladies, are you the famous and

legendary Gospel Sisters!"

The sisters smiled with great amusement

while responding with a resounding, but warm NO!

My girl, or the girl I liked, continued chuckling

beneath her breath even after the subject changed.

"So, do you beautiful ladies have names?"

asked Minister James. I only heard one…

"My name is Thelma Tanner, but you can

call me Thelma. I am from Joliet, Illinois."

"And you, Ministers... Do you have names?"

My God! She is beautiful; more beautiful than any woman I have ever kept company with in the past.

I turn away for a moment to catch my breath...

Just gorgeous! Ooooh weee...

I wasn't referring just to her outward beauty, although her outward beauty is sweeping. Her complexion is the perfect blend of chocolate and smooth cream, just the way I like it. Her hair was full and flowing that night. It was almost too much on a Minister's heart. She was wearing a long, burnt-orange Cashmere coat with a fox fur collar and burnt-orange shoes to match. Her smile is bright as my mother's; and lit me up inside. But it was her voice that really got me.

"My name is Thelma Tanner, but you can call me Thelma."

Umm, umm, ummm... Miss My Name Is Thelma Tanner, But You Can Call Me Thelma. Girl, girl, girl. **My name is Kevin Washington, and you can call me Anytime...**

"Minister... uuuhhh... your name..."

Minister James gave me the elbow again.

"Ah yeah, yeah. My name is Minister Kevin Washington. And rrrrr, yeah you can call me... uuuhh. Yeah, you can call me Minister Kevin Washington, anytime. Yeah, call me Minister Kevin Washington, anytime at all. That's my name. I will answer – Anytime. Yup."

Thelma was bursting at the seams with laughter. It was phenomenal and flowed from her heart straight to mine.

She spoke in a way that resonated in my spirit. She was serious about God. Not a gold-digger, or someone that will try to be with a man just for material gains. She didn't strike me as the kind of person that would walk away in times of adversity. I don't know how I knew these things

264

about her right away like that, but I did. Her conversation was sober, yet lighthearted. I could listen to her for the rest of my life.

She had a way of enunciating her words that gave me goosebumps. I had never heard a woman speak so elegantly before. It reminded me of someone from another country. She was prim and proper, and exotic.

THELMA...

Wow! This girl has me going. I am going to need some oxygen. Lord, help me! Kevin, pull yourself together, man. Don't blow this.

"So, Ministers," one of the other sisters said, "Are either of you married?" asking with grave sincerity and curiosity.

"As a matter of fact, we are not." We held out our hands and began wiggling our fingers. I looked Thelma right in the face and continued wiggling, putting emphasis upon my ring finger while smiling at her.

"See, no rings, ladies."

They giggled again.

"Why did you ask us such a personal question?" I focused on Thelma. I wanted to hear what she had to say. I wanted to hear her voice, see her lips move. See her smile. And figure out what kind of person she really was.

"To be honest," Thelma said, "The guys in the church can't be trusted. They play too many games. And I am sick of it. These church guys act worse than the guys in the street. Just because they show up here in their three-piece suits with a flashy tie and gold or diamond cuff links, doesn't mean they are saved, or even decent people. I've seen it too many times... get a nice young lady, then dog her out. Many of them come to these big events because they know many single church girls will be in attendance. And, a lot of these brothers are already married. We don't want to get caught up in their mess, or yours, if you play those same games. So, we usually ask upfront. If you are married, we do not want to entertain your conversation at all."

"Wow! You said a mouth full. Thank you for sharing that. First, let me apologize for every fake brother that has ever approached you. And you are right. Many guys bring the street with them. And that is wrong. So, we understand your concerns," I said. "But I also want you to consider this. Not all guys are dishonest, Thelma Tanner, But You Can Call Me Thelma. It will be unfair to stereotype all guys based on a few knuckleheads and bad experiences. And it will definitely interfere with God blessing you with a mate because you may not be open because of personal suspicions. I'm truly sorry that you had to experience that. But I want you to know that there are still some good men left."

Playfully, Minister Gamble and I started pointing back and forth at one another, teasing around with the ladies. "Good men, good men.

Yup, yup, yup. That's us." I wiggled my fingers again back in Thelma's direction.

The girls giggled. WE LAUGHED.

After that exchange, it was getting late, and the crowd in the auditorium was starting to wane.

"Well, Ms. Thelma, it was nice meeting you, and the rest of you beautiful young ladies. We have a long day tomorrow. Hopefully, we will see each other in service," I said.

"That would be nice," Thelma said.

We parted ways...

"Man, Minister Gamble, that was nice. I would like to see that young lady again. I am going to pray and ask God to allow me to see her again..."

November 10, 1987 brought on a new development. I woke up with Thelma on my mind. However, another young lady found her way into my radar. She was absolutely gorgeous as well. She was on The Special K like back in the day was today. She told me she was from Kentucky and attended one of the associate congregations in that area. She was twenty-five years old and had two children from a previous relationship, a girl and a boy, ages six and four, respectively. She was very bold. She told me that she had been saved a short time and wanted to get married soon. She brought back that old feeling. I began conversing with her about the Convocation and exchanging stories about our Christian walk. She didn't seem that interested but nodded politely and smiled a lot.

I couldn't get Thelma Tanner, But You Can Call Me Thelma's laugh out of my mind. It was brisk as the lemon tea brewed in grandma's kitchen. While speaking with this young lady, all I could think about was Thelma's smile. I thought about her hair, her hat, her hands. I saw her fingers. I saw her ring finger. It called my name. I saw the way she walked away last night after we ended our exchange. Thelma had a nice walk, and I knew that I never wanted her to walk away from me again. I saw everything about her. I needed to see her again. The other young lady wasn't doing it for me. She paled in comparison to Thelma.

Lord, please let me see Thelma again.

While speaking with the other young lady, I prayed to see Thelma again. However, there were so many people at the Convocation, it was virtually impossible to see anyone twice.

Later that night, I went to another musical. To my surprise, Thelma was just a few pews in front of me to the left, singing with all her might, at the top of her lungs. I laughed so hard.

Why is my heart thumping so hard at the sight of this woman? Jesus... Thank you, God, for allowing me to see her again. You are so faithful, and she is simply gorgeous.

The other young lady was in the service as well, but on the other side of the congregation. She, however, made sure I saw her. She turned her neck in my direction every few minutes. I wasn't trying to be mean, but I postured my body so I wouldn't have to see her.

I didn't get into the service at all that night. But not because of her. I couldn't shake that thumping feeling in my heart. I was busy trying to see what Thelma was doing.

Will she shout...

Will she look back and to her right and see me watching her...

Will she smile when she sees me...

Thelma. Mmm, mmm, mmm. Thelma.

Will she see the other lady stretching her neck...?

Will they fight over me...?

THELMA...

I could barely wait for the service to be over so that I could rush to her. However, we did not get a chance to talk to each other that night; Thelma left the auditorium right away. But, we did see each other at the end of service and trade a saintly wave waaaaaaay from across the room.

JESUS...

My heart leaped and sank all at the same time. I wanted to hear her voice again. I wanted to look at her face. I wanted to be in her face, in her presence.

JESUS...

Despite my wrestling emotions, I knew I must wait on God. Destiny would bring us together the very next day, November 11, 1987, during the communion service.

I was standing in line to buy a tape of the services that week! Thelma came up from out of nowhere.

"Hey, Anytime."

I looked around, saw it was her, and laughed...

"Would you buy a tape for me?" she said. "The line is so long..." She shoved her hand in her purse, stirred around in that massive thing and came up with a $20.

"Wow! Is that a purse or pocketbook or something? Or is it a piece of carryon luggage? What do you have in that thing anyway?"

She laughed. "Wow! Just stop! You are so funny! Here, purchase my tape, please. She pushed the $20 back toward my hands.

My heart was throbbing again.

This was the ideal time, the opportunity, the moment I had prayed for. Here goes...

"Let me take care of it for you. If you don't mind, please put your money back in your camper that you are carrying around. I'd love to purchase the tape for you."

She laughed again.

I loved seeing her laugh.

"No worries. I got you."

"Alright," she said.

And that was that.

"Do you mind if I share my testimony with you?" I asked her.

"Not at all!" She said with excitement. "I would absolutely love to hear your testimony!"

From the time we were in line getting tapes of the service, until after the communion service, we spent four hours together in the lobby talking.

Thelma was floored to learned that I had recently been in a life-altering accident.

"You are a walking miracle. My God!"

"Yes, I am. Thank you for saying that! I'm glad you said that."

"And since you were kind enough to share your testimony, may I please share a small portion of my testimony with you?"

"By all means, sister, yes! Share away."

"Great, and thank you. I lost my brother in the same year that you had your accident, on Thanksgiving Day. It is still difficult to accept that he is really gone. And now, the loss of my aunt just compounds the pain in our family. It's like we are experiencing back to back tragedy."

"I'm really sorry for your loss, Thelma."

"Thank you, Minister Washington. He was the twin of my sister. It hit the family hard. And you know my sister was devastated. He left too soon."

"Oh wow! How did he die?"

"He was in a car crash, just like you. But that day was the last day for him. But praise God for you! You don't look like what you have been through. You are living proof that God will bring you through the storm."

"Wow! Thank you for saying that. It takes a lot of courage and strength to rejoice with someone, especially when you are in pain. I really thank you for saying that. It means a lot."

"Sure. I'm actually here with family in Cleveland, Mississippi. My father's sister passed away and I am here for her services. Since I will be here all week, I thought I'd stop by and enjoy some of the services of the Holy Convocation."

"That's great, Thelma. May God bless you for your faithfulness."

"Absolutely. We must go on, because life goes on. If I stop and shut down, live will bulldoze me. The news of my brother was terrible. However, to see you standing here before me, walking and talking, is a miracle of God. It truly is an amazing thing! The way you describe how critical your injuries were... My God! I don't know if I could have borne seeing my brother go through all of that. Who gets up from paralysis as soon as you did, and with a broken back? Who walks around without a cane the way you are walking right now? Who does that while they are still in the early stages of their healing process? Who? No one that I know! This lets me know that God is in control and you are a medical miracle. My brother didn't make it, but you did. I'm glad that you made it, Minister. Your life really touches my heart."

Thelma began digging around in the yacht that she was carrying on her arm and pulled out a small pack of Kleenex.

"Excuse me for one moment please, Minister."

She opened the small package of tissue, turned to the side and wiped her watering eyes.

"Sister, are you okay?" I reached out and gently touched her shoulder.

"Sure, I'm fine. Oooh Jesus. I got a little misty for a moment. But yes, I'm okay."

My home pastor happened to walk by and saw us talking. He slowed down his pace and watched our interaction intently. I did not acknowledge him at that time.

Thelma and I connected in such a deep, meaningful way. I could feel our hearts being knit together. Our emotions were inflamed. Our hearts were fusing together passionately. I had relationships with other young ladies in the past, but never had I felt myself drawn to any of them the way I was drawn to Thelma. I felt my heart meshing with hers. It was a spiritual connection.

The spiritual connection was stronger than anything I felt as a natural man.

A few hours later, my Pastor passed by us again and saw that we were still engaged in a fervent conversation. Sometime after the Convocation he told me that he could see that something was developing between me and that young lady.

Thelma and I had so many things in common. But most of all, we loved the Lord, and wanted the mate that God had chosen for us. We felt that God's Hand was pulling the strings on our chance meeting. I did not go there looking for a girl to date. But I was smitten.

The timing and conditions were the worst possible. With my accident still being fairly new, I still had so much unfinished business surrounding it. Her life was hectic as well. We had a lot on our plates, but we both felt that it was fate. The attraction was so much more that physical.

It was as God was drawing us out of chaos to the greatest call of our lives. We were being summoned from a life of pain to a precious life of prosperity together.

I felt like I was 10 feet tall and the richest man in the world! I had finally hit the jackpot for sure!

"Look, Thelma... I heard you loud and clear the other night. I don't play games. I am a game changer. So, I'm going to put it out there because I am serious."

"Okay, I don't play games either." Thelma said. "Speak what's in your heart."

"Well, I really like you. I learned a lot in these few hours that we have spent together. I am from Pennsylvania, and you are from Illinois. I am willing, and interested, in engaging in a long-term relationship with you, even if it has to be long-distance. That is, if you are willing to enter into such an agreement with me."

"If you are serious. I am." Thelma said.

"Oh, trust me. I am so serious."

"Well, that great to hear, Minister Washington. You can take it from here. I would love to enter into a relationship with you."

I LAUGHED LIKE A MAN AGAIN...

"Alright. Alright. Okay, yes, great, great, great, great. That's good. I can take it from here. May I start by asking for your phone number and address?"

"No problem. Just make sure you have your Bible when you call."

Thelma and I exchanged phone numbers and addresses! And that was the beginning of our long-distance courtship! During our courtship, I'd call Thelma twice a week; and yes, it was expensive! We'd talk for hours. And, every time we spoke, I had my Bible in my hand. We read Scriptures and prayed together each call, as well as talked about our future life together. I wrote lots of letters... over one hundred, to be exact. And I always had something new and exciting to share with her. The letters and the phone calls, along with the flowers, candy and other acts of affection brought about a pressing question. I asked...

"Do you really believe in our future?"

"What do you mean," she replied?

"Do you believe that you can talk into the future?"

"No, I don't believe that I can do that. No one can, unless they are prophesying."

"Well, I believe they can, and I am not talking about prophesying either."

"Okaaaay, explain to me what you are saying...."

"Absolutely. What time is it there in Joliet?"

"11:30 p.m."

"What day?"

"Friday, of course," she said chuckling. I laughed along with her.

"Well, it's 12:30 a.m., Saturday morning, here in Harrisburg, Pennsylvania.

"Ooooh! I get it. You are Eastern Standard Time. We are Central Standard time! Nice!"

LAUGHING IN MY DEEP MAN VOICE...

"Yep! You get it. So, you see, not only are you talking into the future... **YOU ARE TALKING TO YOUR FUTURE!**"

This confirmed what I had previously told her... "I am your future, and Thelma, you are my future."

This lasted for five months; we were engaged the sixth month, May 30, 1988; and we were married September 17, 1988. And after 30 years and counting, she still does it for me.

I love you, Thelma. Thank you for giving me four wonderful children, one daughter, and three sons. I am a man most blessed in this life. I can't ask God for more. In you, He has made all my dreams come true. Thank you for loving me. Amen.

Family Pictorial Solute

Our Love Grows

*"Lo, children are an heritage of the Lord:
and the fruit of the womb is his reward. As arrows are in
the hand of a mighty man; so are children of the youth.
Happy is the man that hath his quiver full of them..."*

Psalms 127:3-5

Thelma,

Of all the amazing gifts you have given me over the

years, these four are the most precious. Thank you

so much for a quiver full of love!

Love,

Your Future...

Ms. Te'ressa N. Washington-Jackson

Praise Dance Instructor/Author

Te'ressa is the only girl! Our Princess. She is our first born, and she is very gifted. Te'ressa is a determined, ambitious, and sound daughter. She is the first homeschool graduate with Distinguished Honors. Te'ressa is an anointed praise & worship dancer with national and international notoriety. She has traveled to the Bahamas, Las Vegas, Illinois, and Philadelphia thus far in her life. She is highly sought after to perform for civic and ecumenical services and events. Te'ressa is currently pursuing her college degree in elementary education with a minor in dance.

Mr. Kevin N. Washington Jr. (KJ)

Professional Photo-Pro Wrestling
WWA4-Training

Kevin is our champion! He is the second born and his talents are apparent. Kevin is focused, considerate, commands respect, and sets high goals for himself. He is the second homeschool graduate with honors. Kevin has a strong passion and aptitude for graphic arts design. He is an anointed drummer and has played in his local church during revivals and other special services. He has many years of martial arts training and has won multiple awards and trophies for sparring as well as wrestling. He wants to obtain his college education and degree in Graphic Arts Design and Film.

Mr. Kalann L. Washington

Messiah College Wrestling Recruit
NHSCA All American and a District 3AAA Qualifier

Kalann is our scholar! He is the third born and intellectually exceptional. Kalann is methodical, patient, competitive, and appreciative of challenges. He, too, is homeschooled and an honor student. Kalann has a strong interest in Engineering and Psychology. He is an aspiring guitar player and has won multiple awards and trophies for his martial arts competitions. His future is promising with ambitions of becoming a doctor, engineer or psychologist.

Mr. Karrington L. Washington

Messiah College Wrestling Recruit
Varsity Wrestler 197 Pounds
Outstanding Artist & Painter

Karrington is our Peace Maker! He is the fourth born and is full of gifts and talents. Karrington is watchful, a good listener, friendly, and adjusts well to changes. He, too, earned the status of honor student in homeschool. He has exceptional artistic and painting skills. Karrington has excelled in both martial arts and wrestling. He enjoys his family and aspires to become an entrepreneur when he graduates from college.

287

This Is My Story

In October 2017, I was two months into my junior year at Messiah College. The year started with lots of excitement and much to look forward to. As an English Education Major, coordinator for a youth outreach program on behalf of Messiah's Agape Center volunteering services in Harrisburg, and a collegiate athlete on Messiah's wrestling team, I always had something to do... and I loved it.

One day, after a session of weightlifting, I started noticing minor gastrointestinal pain and discomfort. I assumed it was soreness from deadlifting or a reaction to food I had eaten; however, the pain persisted and slowly worsened into a much greater issue. I was forced to eliminate most foods from my diet. I began to experience excruciating abdominal pain when moving and sleeping, falling down on the ground from fatigue, and rapid weight loss that would land me in the hospital. I went from feeling my strongest—weighing 205 pounds and deadlifting over 400 pounds—in October, to weighing less than 154 pounds and needing a cane to walk by May 24th.

Its impact on me

 I started to notice symptoms early in October, but I was officially diagnosed in December of 2017 after a colonoscopy. I was told I had **Ulcerative colitis**. I didn't quite know what that meant. Ulcerative colitis is an autoimmune disorder and categorized as a type of **Irritable Bowel Disease,** much like Crohn's, however, characterized by chronic inflammation in the colon. According to the Cleveland Clinic, people with severely active UC have a minimum of six or more bloody bowel movements a day. In addition, from personal experience, severe symptoms also included abdominal cramping, anemia, nausea, fatigue, and insomnia. Factors like environment, genetics, and diet play a big role in the development of UC, but no single or primary cause is yet known.

Over the course of the school year, the severity of my condition fluctuated, with frequent jumps between drug prescriptions, recommendations, and hidden food allergies. Overall, my health was declining. Between the side effects from the medications and the symptoms of the disease, my involvements academically, athletically, occupationally, and socially, steadily declined.

Turn for the worst

Near the end of my spring semester, dealing with UC during school was an uphill battle. My doctors, family, and support systems tried to help as much as they could, but my condition was getting worse. Right before final exams in May, I experienced my worst-flare up to date.

The severity of my symptoms resulted in multiple hospital stays, causing my withdrawal from classes and the rest of my student activities. My hospital visits during this period consisted of two overnight blood transfusions for anemia, as well as a two-week stay at Penn State Hershey Medical Center during the worst flare-up.

There were only two options left. The first was a dual treatment with an immunosuppressant drug named Remicade and more of a corticosteroid, Prednisone; both had lots of long-term, potentially harmful, side effects. My second option was a colectomy: the **removal** of my colon, and replacement with an external colostomy bag. Imagine that: a 20-year-old student-athlete being told his options were to shut down his immune system, or have his large intestine removed to keep—let alone enjoy—his life.

I was resistant to the suggestions of surgery; however, as my condition became more critical, I became less reluctant to this option. Just as I started to believe that the invasive surgery was my only remaining option, my body began to respond to the IV medications, and the severity of my symptoms slowly began to decrease. After 14 days, I was released from the hospital, but discharge was only the beginning of my recovery.

Present day

It has been almost two months since my discharge, and during this crucial stage I have been recovering. The daily progress might be marginal to some, but the small steps are big leaps to me. Walking, ingesting food, and even brushing my teeth were once impossible without having an adverse reaction.

My outpatient management consists of lots of follow-up appointments with my GI doctor, along with physical therapy and meetings with nutritionists. Instead of trial and error on my own, I have been able to get a better understanding of my condition and slowly get healthier.

While I am catching up on coursework from the spring semester and focusing on progressing in my health, I have been unable to work to cover expenses and save money for the school year. My immune system is suppressed, and my body is not completely stable.

Where there is need
Much like the factors that trigger it, everybody with IBD is different. Due to its complexities, everyone has their own dietary needs, and because of this, malnutrition is common. Through education, advisement from my doctors, support from others, trial (and error), I have learned how important of a role diet plays for recovery. I've had to make radical changes to what I eat, but slowly I've been able to build a healthy and healing lifestyle based on research, and experience. Frequent trips to grocery stores and markets in order to find tolerable foods have been, and continue to be exhausting, both physically and **financially**, on my family and me.

While the prescribed medication I have been taking has helped kick start my body into remission, there is a chance for medication tolerance. Remicade users sometimes build a defense against the medication that helped them, and corticosteroids are known to have adverse and potentially fatal effects for long-term users. I cannot be on the medications forever, so my next stage of recovery is going to be critical.

Where there is hope
Giving my body what it needs to heal is one major step. There are nutrients that can fight inflammation and help aid in repairing the intestinal wall. Some of the best sources of healing nutrition are amino acids, proteins, bone broths, lean

meats, vegetables, and a personal list of food that is slowly growing based on sound research.

For my final year as a senior, the need extends beyond just nutritional health. Raising $3000 will cover the cost of books and school expenses, tuition, and other needed supplies come September 1st. This also would cover transportation to doctor visits and checkups, as well as therapy and recovery. During this period, I've had a lot to be thankful for. There have been people who have reached out to me in support, some of whom I've never met before! Many have continued to ask how they can be a support through this process. This is how...

Whether through prayer, monetary support, reaching out to connect about the UC condition, or even providing some gardening tips, support can come in many ways. A well-rounded approach to a difficult condition is how I'm approaching this obstacle in my life. I appreciate anyone who supports me and others on this journey.